# Introduction to Property-Casualty Insurance

# Introduction to Property-Casualty Insurance

Edited by
Arthur L. Flitner, CPCU, ARM

2nd Edition • 1st Printing

**The Institutes**
720 Providence Road, Suite 100
Malvern, Pennsylvania 19355-3433

Unless otherwise apparent, examples used in The Institutes materials related to this course are based on hypothetical situations and are for educational purposes only. The characters, persons, products, services, and organizations described in these examples are fictional. Any similarity or resemblance to any other character, person, product, services, or organization is merely coincidental. The Institutes are not responsible for such coincidental or accidental resemblances.

This material may contain Internet Web site links external to The Institutes. The Institutes neither approve nor endorse any information, products, or services to which any external Web sites refer. Nor do The Institutes control these Web sites' content or the procedures for Web site content development.

The Institutes specifically disclaim any implied warranties of merchantability or fitness for a particular purpose. No warranty may be created or extended by sales representatives or written sales materials.

The Institutes materials related to this course are provided with the understanding that The Institutes are not engaged in rendering legal, accounting, or other professional service. Nor are The Institutes explicitly or implicitly stating that any of the processes, procedures, or policies described in the materials are the only appropriate ones to use. The advice and strategies contained herein may not be suitable for every situation.



2nd Edition • 1st Printing • September 2011

Library of Congress Control Number: 2011906566

ISBN 978-0-89463-466-6

# Foreword

The Institutes are the trusted leader in delivering proven knowledge solutions that drive powerful business results for the risk management and property-casualty insurance industry. For more than 100 years, The Institutes have been meeting the industry's changing professional development needs with customer-driven products and services.

In conjunction with industry experts and members of the academic community, our Knowledge Resources Department develops our course and program content, including Institutes study materials. Practical and technical knowledge gained from Institutes courses enhances qualifications, improves performance, and contributes to professional growth—all of which drive results.

The Institutes' proven knowledge helps individuals and organizations achieve powerful results with a variety of flexible, customer-focused options:

**Recognized Credentials**—The Institutes offer an unmatched range of widely recognized and industry-respected specialty credentials. The Institutes' Chartered Property Casualty Underwriter (CPCU) professional designation is designed to provide a broad understanding of the property-casualty insurance industry. Depending on professional needs, CPCU students may select either a commercial insurance focus or a personal risk management and insurance focus and may choose from a variety of electives.

In addition, The Institutes offer certificate or designation programs in a variety of disciplines, including these:

- Claims
- Commercial underwriting
- Fidelity and surety bonding
- General insurance
- Insurance accounting and finance
- Insurance information technology
- Insurance production and agency management
- Insurance regulation and compliance
- Management
- Marine insurance
- Personal insurance
- Premium auditing
- Quality insurance services
- Reinsurance
- Risk management
- Surplus lines

**Flexible Online Learning**—The Institutes have an unmatched variety of technical insurance content covering topics from accounting to underwriting, which we now deliver through hundreds of online courses. These cost-effective self-study courses are a convenient way to fill gaps in technical knowledge in a matter of hours without ever leaving the office.

**Continuing Education**—A majority of The Institutes' courses are filed for CE credit in most states. We also deliver quality, affordable, online CE courses quickly and conveniently through our newest business unit, CEU.com. Visit www.CEU.com to learn more.

**College Credits**—Most Institutes courses carry college credit recommendations from the American Council on Education. A variety of courses also qualify for credits toward certain associate, bachelor's, and master's degrees at several prestigious colleges and universities. More information is available in the Student Services section of our Web site, www.TheInstitutes.org.

**Custom Applications**—The Institutes collaborate with corporate customers to utilize our trusted course content and flexible delivery options in developing customized solutions that help them achieve their unique organizational goals.

**Insightful Analysis**—Our Insurance Research Council (IRC) division conducts public policy research on important contemporary issues in property-casualty insurance and risk management. Visit www.ircweb.org to learn more or purchase its most recent studies.

The Institutes look forward to serving the risk management and property-casualty insurance industry for another 100 years. We welcome comments from our students and course leaders; your feedback helps us continue to improve the quality of our study materials.

Peter L. Miller, CPCU
President and CEO
The Institutes

# Preface

This book is the assigned text for the Introduction to Property-Casualty Insurance course offered by The Institutes. Designed for those who are new to property-casualty insurance, the course enables learners to see how insurance works as both a vital business and a contract for protecting individuals, families, and businesses against the financial consequences of accidental losses.

The opening assignment defines the insurance mechanism, identifies common types of property-casualty insurance, and explains how insurance benefits society. The remaining eight assignments consist of two groupings, corresponding to themes of "insurance as a business" and "insurance as a contract."

The "insurance as a business" assignments introduce the reader to the core functions of insurance organizations: marketing, underwriting, and claims. A short assignment on each function examines its goals, the systems and activities used to reach those goals, and the tools that measure success in reaching those goals. The final assignment in this grouping explains why insurance is regulated and how regulation affects insurance business operations.

The first of the "insurance as a contract" assignments discusses insurance policy structure, the basic types of policy provisions, and a simple method for analyzing policies. The next assignment identifies loss exposures faced by individuals and families and explains how personal insurance policies cover those exposures. The last two assignments show how commercial insurance policies cover the property and liability loss exposures of businesses.

Learners who successfully complete this course acquire a solid base of knowledge that will help them to succeed on the job and in more advanced insurance courses.

The Institutes are grateful to the insurance professionals, course leaders, and course sponsors who provided guidance and review during the planning of this text. Their assistance helped to ensure that the text is accurate and reflects current industry practice.

For more information about The Institutes' programs, please call our Customer Service Department at (800) 644-2101, email us at customerservice@TheInstitutes.org, or visit our Web site at www.TheInstitutes.org.

Arthur L. Flitner

# Contributors

The Institutes acknowledge with deep appreciation the contributions made to the content of this text by the following persons:

Charles Bush

Laura J. Partsch, JD

Judith M. Vaughan, AIC, BA

# Contents

Direct Your Learning

1

# Insurance Overview

## Educational Objectives

After learning the content of this assignment, you should be able to:

- Explain why the concepts of risk, transfer, and pooling are essential to insurance.
- Identify the common types of property-casualty insurance.
- Explain how insurance benefits society.
- Explain how insurers use the premiums they receive.

## Outline

# Insurance Overview

# 1

## WHAT IS INSURANCE?

Many businesses and families have concerns about the possible financial effect of an unforeseen event, such as a fire or an auto accident. Most people know that insurance can help to alleviate some of these concerns by providing a source of payment for the costs of such events.

**Insurance** is a mechanism by which risk is transferred by a person or business to an **insurer**, which reimburses the insured person or business for covered losses and provides for the sharing of losses among all **insureds**. This sharing is possible because the insurer collects a pool of all of the **premiums** paid by customers into a fund from which it pays losses.

The insurance mechanism, therefore, includes three essential components:

- Risk
- Transfer
- Pooling

### Risk

The first component of the insurance mechanism is **risk**. The idea of risk is a fundamental insurance concept. Individuals and families face uncertainty from the possible financial consequences of **loss exposures** such as fire, weather-related, or other damage to their homes and lawsuits or injuries arising from an auto accident. Business owners are concerned about the financial consequences of injuries to customers while on their business premises or to their employees in the course of their jobs. They are also concerned about potential costs arising from physical damage to owned buildings or personal property, loss of profit from an interruption of their business, burglary or robbery, and many other possible loss exposures.

### Transfer

The second component of the insurance mechanism is **transfer**. The financial consequences of unanticipated events can be transferred to an insurer, thus reducing the risk or uncertainty associated with these costs. Losses may still occur, but the insured's uncertainty regarding his or her financial consequences is reduced because a mechanism for paying the costs of these losses has been put into place.

**Insurance**
A risk management technique that transfers the potential financial consequences of certain specified loss exposures from the insured to the insurer.

**Insurer**
A company that sells insurance policies to protect insureds against financial hardship caused by financial losses.

**Insured**
Any person or organization who is insured under an insurance policy.

**Premium**
The price of the insurance coverage provided for a specified period.

**Risk**
The uncertainty about outcomes, some of which can be negative.

**Loss exposure**
Any condition or situation that presents a possibility of loss, whether or not an actual loss occurs.

**Transfer**
In the context of risk management, a risk financing technique by which the financial responsibility for losses and variability in cash flows is shifted to another party.

Insurance policy

A contract that states the agreement between and the rights and duties of the insurer and insured.

For example, when an individual purchases a new home, he or she will purchase an **insurance policy** to reduce the financial uncertainties related to the ownership of that home and to provide for the payment of losses that may occur. When insureds transfer their risk of financial loss to an insurer, they are exchanging the possibility of large, uncertain loss amounts for smaller, more certain premium amounts. Risks are transferred to an insurer through the use of an insurance policy.

## Pooling

Pooling

An arrangement that facilitates the grouping together of loss exposures and the resources to pay for any losses that may occur.

The third component of the insurance mechanism is pooling. Insurers combine all of the premiums collected from customers into a fund that is used to pay losses as they occur. **Pooling** means that all insureds share the costs of each other's losses. In effect, the cost of paying for losses that occur for relatively few insureds is spread among all members of the group.

This method of sharing of costs among all insureds makes each individual's premium relatively small. For example, the premium to insure a family home valued at $350,000 may be only $2,000 per year, even though the policy may pay the entire $350,000 in the event that the house were to be totally destroyed by a covered peril, such as fire. See the exhibit "Risk, Transfer, and Pooling: An Example."

### Risk, Transfer, and Pooling: An Example

Frank has just purchased a new car and is concerned that an auto accident could cause him a large financial loss (risk). Frank pays Insurer A $2,000 to insure his car for one year (transfer). Fortunately, Frank has no accidents during the year. Karla pays Insurer A $2,500 to insure her car for one year. Unfortunately, during a rainstorm that year, Karla's car skids into another car, and Karla is injured. Karla's auto insurance pays $7,450 to repair her car, $8,300 to repair the other car, and $9,000 for Karla's medical bills.

Karla's insurer can pay this loss because it has collected adequate premiums from Frank and many other insureds who did not have losses (pooling). Frank, Karla, and all of the other insureds were willing to pay a premium to transfer their risk to the insurer. In effect, all of the premiums went into a pool from which Karla's loss was paid. In other words, Frank and others shared the cost of Karla's loss.

[DA00418]

Property-casualty insurance

One of the two main sectors of the insurance industry, encompassing numerous types of insurance, most of which cover the financial consequences of damage to one's own property or legal liability to others.

# WHAT IS PROPERTY-CASUALTY INSURANCE?

Many types of property-casualty insurance policies are available to cover the loss exposures of individuals, families, and business organizations.

**Property-casualty insurance** is one of two main sectors of the insurance industry in the United States. The other main sector is life-health insurance.

Most individual insurers provide either property-casualty insurance or life-health insurance, but not both. A group of insurers under common ownership may include both property-casualty insurers and life-health insurers. In this way, the group can meet all the insurance needs of its customers.

The types of property-casualty insurance policies available for individuals, families, and business organizations fall into two categories:

- Personal insurance policies
- Commercial insurance policies

## Personal Insurance Policies

These are common types of personal insurance policies:

- Homeowners
- Personal auto
- Personal watercraft
- Personal umbrella

Personal insurance policies are designed to cover personal loss exposures such as those that arise from buildings, personal property (including contents of the home), physical damage to vehicles, and **legal liability** arising from the ownership of a home, vehicles, or watercraft as well as the activities of individuals and families.

A **homeowners policy** provides both property and liability coverage. The property coverage protects insureds for damage to the home and its contents caused by fire, wind, lightning, and other causes of loss. Most homeowners policies also include coverage for theft of the contents of the home. The homeowners policy also includes **personal liability coverage** for legal liability that may arise if someone is injured while on the property (for example, when a visitor falls down the front steps outside the home or is bitten by the family's dog).

A **personal auto policy (PAP)** covers losses due to bodily injury to another person or damage to property of others arising from an auto accident for which the insured is liable. It also covers damage to the vehicle that results from a collision or from fire, theft, wind, contact with a bird or another animal, and other causes of loss.

The personal liability coverage in the homeowners policy and the auto liability coverage in the PAP exclude or limit coverage for operation of any watercraft. Therefore, a person who owns a boat may need a separate **personal watercraft policy** that covers not only legal liability that may arise from accidents involving the boat, but also physical damage to the boat.

An insured that requires higher limits of insurance than those available under personal liability or personal auto coverage may also purchase a personal **umbrella liability policy**. Typical limits for a personal umbrella policy range

**Legal liability**
The legally enforceable obligation of a person or an organization to pay a sum of money (called damages) to another person or organization.

**Homeowners policy**
Policy that covers most of the property and liability loss exposures that arise out of residential property ownership and occupancy, as well as property and liability loss exposures that individuals and families may have while they are away from their residences.

**Personal liability coverage**
Coverage for damages, plus costs of any defense, related to a claim or suit brought against the insured that resulted from bodily injury or property damage caused by an occurrence covered under the policy.

**Personal auto policy (PAP)**
An insurance policy that covers an individual or a family against loss exposures arising out of the ownership, maintenance, or use of automobiles.

**Personal watercraft policy**
An insurance policy that covers an individual's or a family's loss exposures arising out of the ownership, maintenance, or use of watercraft used principally for recreational or personal transportation purposes.

**Umbrella liability policy**
A liability policy that provides excess coverage above underlying policies and may also provide coverage not available in the underlying policies, subject to a self-insured retention.

Commercial Package Policy (CPP)

Policy that covers two or more lines of business by combining ISO's commercial lines coverage parts.

Businessowners policy (BOP)

A package policy that combines most of the property and liability coverages needed by small and medium-sized businesses.

Commercial property insurance

Insurance that covers commercial buildings and their contents against various types of property loss.

Commercial crime insurance

Insurance that covers (1) money and securities against numerous perils (not limited to crime perils) and (2) property other than money and securities against crime perils, such as employee theft, robbery, theft by outsiders, and extortion.

Commercial general liability (CGL) insurance

Insurance that covers many of the common liability loss exposures faced by an organization, including its premises, operations, and products.

Commercial auto insurance

Insurance that covers a business or a not-for-profit organization against loss exposures arising out of the ownership, maintenance, or use of automobiles.

Workers compensation insurance

Insurance that provides coverage for benefits an employer is obligated to pay under workers compensation laws.

from $1 million to $2 million or more, and they provide an additional level of protection for large liability losses.

## Commercial Insurance Policies

Loss exposures that arise from a business operation are covered under commercial insurance policies. These are common types of commercial insurance:

- Commercial property
- Commercial crime
- Commercial general liability
- Commercial auto
- Workers compensation
- Commercial umbrella

Many business organizations purchase a **commercial package policy (CPP)** or a **businessowners policy (BOP)**. Each of these policies combines the needed property, crime, and liability coverages into one policy.

**Commercial property insurance** covers damage to buildings or their contents that results from fire, vandalism, and other causes of loss.

**Commercial crime insurance** protects against theft of contents such as cash registers, computers, inventory, and other business property and of money that could be stolen in a robbery during business hours or in a burglary that occurs after business hours. Crime insurance also can include employee theft coverage for crimes committed by employees (for example, when an employee steals money or inventory from the business). See the exhibit "Coverages Based on Customers' Needs."

**Commercial general liability (CGL) insurance** protects the insured against claims alleging that the insured is legally liable for bodily injury to others and for damage to the property of others. For example, a retail store could be responsible if a customer falls on the store's wet floor and is injured. Also, if a customer is injured by a product that the store sold, the CGL policy would cover the store's legal liability.

**Commercial auto insurance** protects a business organization against claims for legal liability to others for bodily injury or property damage resulting from the use of vehicles owned or operated by the business. Commercial auto insurance also protects against damage to vehicles as the result of collisions and other accidents.

Because employers are required by law to pay certain benefits to employees who are injured on the job or who contract a job-related disease, business organizations need **workers compensation insurance**, which pays the cost of medical care, lost wages, and other benefits as specified by state law. These benefits are payable regardless of who caused the injury or illness.

## Coverages Based on Customers' Needs

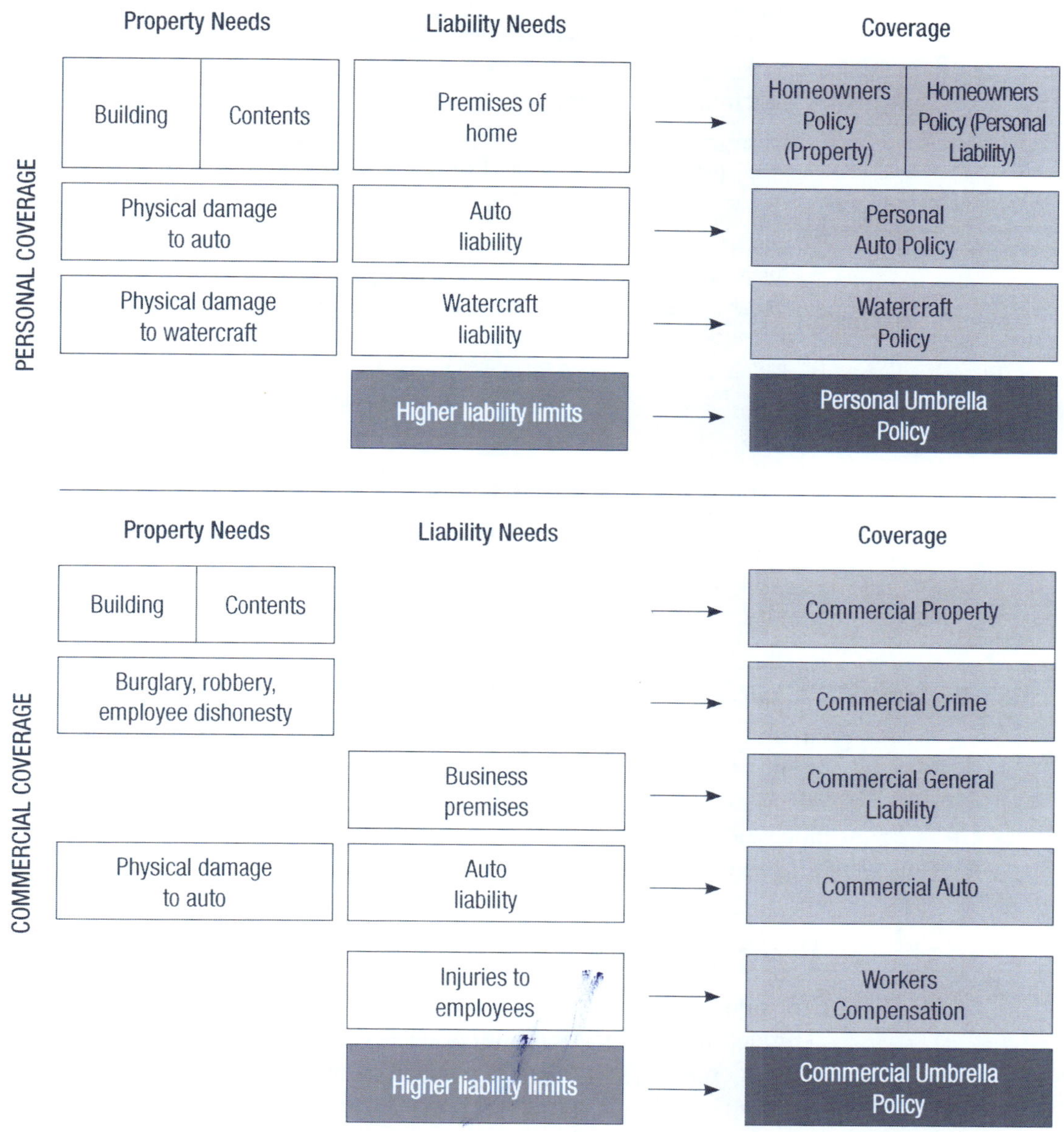


[DA00421]

A commercial umbrella liability policy, which is similar to the personal umbrella policy, provides additional limits beyond those provided by the CGL, commercial auto, and other policies, protecting the insured in the event of a large liability loss. See the exhibit "Types of Insurance Policies—An Example."

**Types of Insurance Policies—An Example**

Rob and his wife, Laurie, own a sandwich shop in a suburban shopping center. They also own a home and two cars. Rob and Laurie are concerned that damage to their business or home could result in substantial financial loss. They have contacted their insurance agent to discuss these concerns and to design an insurance program to meet their personal and commercial needs.

The insurance agent will determine Rob and Laurie's insurance policy needs by examining their loss exposures. Because Rob and Laurie have both personal and commercial loss exposures, they will need both personal and commercial insurance policies.

The personal insurance policies will cover losses arising out of Rob and Laurie's personal loss exposures related to the ownership of the home and cars. For loss exposures arising from the sandwich shop, Rob and Laurie will need commercial insurance policies.

[DA00422]

# HOW DOES INSURANCE BENEFIT SOCIETY?

The property-casualty insurance industry is a multibillion-dollar industry that not only employs millions of people, but also provides numerous benefits to society.

The primary benefit is that, through insurance, individuals and businesses are reimbursed for the costs of covered losses. This loss payment allows individuals and families to recover quickly and businesses to continue operations. A related benefit is that uncertainty about potential future losses is reduced. In addition to loss payment and reducing uncertainty, other benefits of insurance include using resources efficiently, promoting risk control, satisfying legal requirements, and providing a basis for credit.

## Paying Losses

The major benefit of insurance is indemnifying insureds for covered losses. Through indemnification, individuals and businesses are able to maintain their economic position and avoid becoming a burden on others. For example, when a family's house is destroyed by fire and the loss is covered under an insurance policy, the family will be less dependent on relatives or government organizations for lodging or other continuing expenses.

When a business suffers a large loss that is covered under an insurance policy, the business may avoid bankruptcy. Also, the business contributes to society because it can continue to provide jobs for employees, products for its customers, and business for its suppliers. By providing loss payments, insurance contributes to the continued financial strength and stability of individuals, families, and businesses while reducing the uncertainty about future losses.

## Reducing Uncertainty

Another benefit of insurance, which is closely related to paying for losses, is the reduction of uncertainty that insurance protection provides. An individual or a family will have increased peace of mind knowing that the possible financial consequences of losses arising from the ownership of a home or a car will be covered by insurance.

Likewise, entrepreneurs can establish new businesses knowing that the uncertainties related to the financial consequences of some events will be reduced through the purchase of insurance coverage. Existing businesses will be more likely to expand into new operations knowing that insurance coverage is in place for such events. This expansion will benefit society by increasing employment for that business and for businesses in the same community that are providers of services and supplies.

## Using Resources Efficiently

When individuals and businesses purchase insurance policies, they are, in effect, exchanging small, certain premium amounts for possibly much larger, unknown loss amounts. Insurance makes it unnecessary for individuals and businesses to set aside large amounts of money to pay for the financial consequences of losses that can be insured. Money that would otherwise be set aside to pay for possible losses can be used to improve a family's quality of life or to contribute to the growth of a business.

For example, instead of establishing a fund to pay for future losses such as wind damage to buildings or lawsuits resulting from falls on the premises, a business can purchase an insurance policy that will provide a source of payment for such events. When a family purchases a homeowners policy, it avoids the need to set aside a large sum, perhaps $50,000, in savings to be used in the event the house is damaged by fire or other causes of loss. Instead, the family can spend $1,500 for an insurance policy and then use the rest of the $50,000 in savings for another purpose, such as college tuition or retirement savings funds.

## Promoting Risk Control

Insurers are interested in lowering the costs of losses and, therefore, promote a variety of risk control activities to their insureds by providing premium reductions for those insureds who practice risk control. These risk control activities can either lower the frequency of potential accidents by preventing losses from happening (loss prevention) or reduce the severity of accidents that occur despite loss prevention activities (loss reduction).

For example, individuals and businesses can use fire and burglar alarms to prevent property and crime losses from occurring. Smoke detectors or sprinklers can assist in reducing property losses, and driver training programs can help to reduce the severity of auto losses.

Society benefits when losses are controlled because lives are saved and property is preserved. Controlling losses reduces the amount of money insurers must pay out in claims, which allows insurers to reduce insurance costs to all of their customers.

## Satisfying Legal Requirements

Insurance is often used or required to satisfy legal requirements. In many states, for example, owners of automobiles must prove that they have auto liability insurance before they can register their autos. All states have laws that require employers to pay for job-related injuries or illnesses of their employees, and employers generally purchase workers compensation insurance to meet this financial obligation.

## Providing a Basis for Credit

Insurance is important in the use of credit in our economy. Most banks require property insurance on a home before they will provide a mortgage to help the buyer pay for the home. Banks and leasing companies also require evidence of automobile physical damage insurance before approving an auto loan or a lease agreement for a vehicle. When a business applies for a loan to purchase inventory or production equipment, the lender might require the borrower to show that the property is insured before approving the loan.

# HOW DO INSURERS USE THE PREMIUMS THEY RECEIVE?

Insurers collect billions of dollars in premiums each year for the policies they issue to their customers. As a result, insurance customers are often curious about how those premium dollars are used.

Insurers use premium dollars in three principal ways:

- To pay claims for insured losses
- To pay expenses for running the insurance operation
- To invest premium dollars that are not immediately needed

## Pay Claims

One way in which insurers use collected premiums is claim payment. The primary reason that customers purchase insurance coverage is for payment of covered losses. If a loss occurs, the insured files a claim with the insurer. The insurer's claim department is responsible for investigating the circumstances of the loss and paying the claim, if covered by the policy. Property insurance claims are generally straightforward and can usually be settled promptly.

Liability insurance claims often involve a lawsuit, trial, and other legal proceedings, which can last for many months or, in some cases, several years. This extended period of time and the involvement of attorneys increase the expenses related to settling liability claims. A large portion of the premiums insurers collect are used to pay the losses and the expenses related to claim settlement.

## Pay Expenses

A second way in which insurers use collected premiums is paying expenses for running the insurance operation. A portion of the collected premiums is used to cover expenses related to selling, issuing, and servicing the policies sold by the insurer. When a policy is sold through an independent agent, the insurer pays commissions to that agent.

Also, once an application has been submitted to the insurer, many of the insurer's staff are involved in processing the application, issuing a policy, and then providing ongoing customer service once the policy has been issued. The insurer must pay the salaries of underwriters who review applications for acceptability, rating staff who calculate premiums, and processing staff who provide ongoing service to policyholders.

In addition to paying employee salaries and benefits, insurers have the same types of operating expenses that any other business would have. These expenses include rent or mortgage payments, utilities, taxes, advertising, and similar business-related expenses.

## Investments

A third way in which insurers use premiums is in investments. An important aspect of the insurance mechanism is that policyholders pay premiums at the start of the policy period, before any losses have happened. Because future loss amounts cannot be predicted with complete accuracy, insurers must build a fund or reserves for the payment of losses in the future. Insurers invest the premium dollars that are not immediately needed to pay losses or expenses.

An insurance operation is considered profitable when the total premiums collected by the insurer are greater than the amounts paid for losses and for all expenses. In those years when the insurance operation earns a profit, any money that remains after losses and expenses have been paid is used to build a fund for contingencies (such as an unanticipated catastrophic hurricane or other losses that exceed loss projections) and also to pay dividends to the insurer's stockholders or policyholders.

In other years, when the insurance operation fails to earn a profit, insurers may use investment income to offset losses that exceed premiums collected in a given year. This approach allows insurers to make an operating profit by using investment income to offset those loss amounts that exceed collected premium amounts.

## SUMMARY

The concepts of risk, transfer, and pooling are critical components of the insurance mechanism. These three concepts form a foundation on which the insurance mechanism is based.

Many types of property-casualty insurance policies cover personal and commercial loss exposures. The loss exposures of individuals and families are mainly related to their residences, personal vehicles, or owned watercraft. Common types of personal insurance policies are, therefore, homeowners, personal auto policies (PAP), and watercraft policies.

Commercial insurance policies include commercial property coverage, commercial crime, and commercial general liability (CGL) coverage. These coverages are often combined into a single commercial package policy (CPP) or a businessowners policy (BOP). Other common commercial insurance policies include commercial auto, workers compensation, and commercial umbrella.

Insurance provides many benefits to society as a whole and to individuals and businesses. The primary benefit is that insurance provides a mechanism to pay for the financial consequences of losses. Also, because insurance allows for the payment of losses, a related benefit is the reduction of uncertainty regarding how losses, particularly large loss amounts, will be paid. Other benefits of insurance include using resources efficiently, promoting risk control, satisfying legal requirements, and providing a basis for credit.

Every year, insurers collect large amounts of premium dollars from their customers. In return, the insurers promise to pay for any future losses covered under the policies. In addition to using premiums to pay losses, insurers must also pay expenses related to paying claims and operating the business. Insurers also invest funds that are not immediately needed to pay losses or expenses.

# Direct Your Learning

# 2

## Insurance Functions: Marketing

### Educational Objectives

After learning the content of this assignment, you should be able to:

- Distinguish among the following insurance functions:
  - Marketing
  - Underwriting
  - Claims
  - Risk control
  - Premium audit
- Describe the role of each of the following parties in an insurance transaction:
  - Insured
  - Insurer
  - Producer
- Given a description of an insurance producer's or an insurer's operations, identify the insurance marketing system(s) being used.
- Given a case about an insurance producer, identify the producer job functions being performed or that need to be performed.

### Outline

# Insurance Functions: Marketing

# 2

## OVERVIEW OF INSURANCE FUNCTIONS

Insurers perform many functions to provide products and services to their customers.

Insurers sell insurance policies and pay claims as required by those policies, but they do much more. They perform multiple key functions in order to accomplish their goal of protecting their customers while earning a profit:

- Marketing
- Underwriting
- Claims
- Risk control
- Premium audit

Many insurers have a department for each of these functions. Some insurers may outsource some functions, and others combine several functions within a department. Insurers may use different terms for these functions than those used here.

Each of these functions contributes to or detracts from the overall effectiveness of the insurer, depending on how well it is performed. The functions must also interact with each other; their efficient interaction is vital to the survival and continued success of an insurer.

### Marketing

Marketing involves determining the products or services customers want and need and delivering them to those customers. The marketing function contributes significantly to an insurer's profit goals and its goals of meeting customers' needs. The insurer cannot make a profit if it does not provide products and services the customer needs.

An insurer will likely include these elements in a successful marketing program:

- Using market research to determine the needs of potential customers
- Advertising to inform customers about the insurer's products and services
- Selecting appropriate marketing systems
- Training to prepare the sales force to meet the customer's needs

- Setting sales goals and implementing strategies for achieving them
- Motivating and managing the sales force

## Underwriting

Underwriting

The process of selecting insureds, pricing coverage, determining insurance policy terms and conditions, and then monitoring the underwriting decisions made.

Underwriter

An insurer employee who evaluates applicants for insurance, selects those that are acceptable to the insurer, prices coverage, and determines policy terms and conditions.

The role of the **underwriting** function is to determine what loss exposures will be insured, for what amount of coverage, at what price, and under what conditions. **Underwriters** typically follow the underwriting process, which involves gathering the necessary information, making the underwriting decision, and implementing that decision.

Underwriters must carry out a variety of activities to apply the underwriting process. These examples of underwriting activities are central to the underwriting process:

- Selecting insureds
- Pricing coverage
- Determining policy terms and conditions

Underwriters carefully screen potential insureds to determine which ones to insure. They make their selections by applying the underwriting criteria set by the insurer to the loss exposures of customers who have applied for insurance policies. A successful underwriting function ensures that those applicants who are selected receive the level of coverage that adequately reflects their loss exposures at the appropriate price.

After selecting insureds, underwriting determines the price for the insurance. The goal is to charge a premium that is commensurate with the loss exposure. In other words, each insured's premium should be set at a level that is adequate to enable the total premiums paid by a large group of similar insureds to pay the losses and expenses of that group and to allow the insurer to achieve a reasonable profit.

Selection of insureds and pricing of coverage are intertwined with a third underwriting activity—determining policy terms and conditions, which requires certain circumstances to occur or not occur before coverage will apply to a loss. An insurer must decide exactly what policy terms and conditions of coverage it will offer each applicant. For example, an insurer may be willing to add flood coverage to a commercial property policy if the insured building is not located in a high-hazard flood zone.

## Claims

Claim

A demand by a person or business seeking to recover from an insurer for a loss that may be covered by an insurance policy.

Insurers expect to pay **claims**. Without claims, insurance would be unnecessary. When policyholders purchase insurance, they are buying protection for the potential financial consequences of covered losses. The insurer promises to make payments to or on behalf of the insured for covered losses. The claim function is responsible for keeping this promise to the insured by providing prompt and professional loss adjustment services.

Because more than half of what insurers spend goes to the claim function, its proper and efficient performance is important to an insurer's profitability. When evaluating a claim, the adjuster typically applies a claim handling process that includes these six activities:

1. Acknowledging a claim and assigning it to a claim representative
2. Identifying the policy
3. Contacting the insured or the insured's representative
4. Investigating and documenting the claim
5. Determining cause of loss and loss amount
6. Concluding the claim

The purpose of the claim handling process is to achieve a fair and equitable settlement based on the circumstances of the loss. Loss settlements that are too high increase the cost of insurance for everybody. Loss settlements that are too low deprive the insured of the full benefits of the insurance policy. Paying inadequate loss settlements also diminishes the insurer's business reputation and can negatively affect the marketing function.

## Risk Control

The primary purpose of an insurer's **risk control** function is to prevent or reduce losses, if possible. From an economic viewpoint, controlling losses is preferable to insuring losses because it reduces the waste of valuable resources. As a practical matter, both insuring and controlling losses are likely to be used jointly for most large loss exposures, because preventing all losses is seldom possible.

Risk control

A conscious act or decision not to act that reduces the frequency and/or severity of losses or makes losses more predictable.

The risk control function supports underwriters in selecting which loss exposures to insure. Risk control representatives can provide information to underwriters beyond what the application provides. For example, field inspection reports on an applicant's premises and operations can provide important details about the applicant's loss exposures that are not apparent on the application.

An insurer's risk control representatives also provide a valuable service for insureds by helping them prevent losses or reduce their effect. For example, a risk control representative can provide expert advice concerning sprinkler systems for fire suppression.

## Premium Audit

Another insurer function is the **premium audit** function. Many commercial insurance policies are written subject to audit because the premium amount is calculated using a loss exposure measurement that can change during the

Premium audit

Methodical examination of a policyholder's operations, records, and books of account to determine the actual exposure units and premium for insurance coverages already provided.

policy period, which is often one year. The purpose of the audit, which occurs at the end of a policy period, is to determine any adjustments to the premium that may be required based on the insured's actual loss exposures during that period.

For example, the premium of a workers compensation policy that pays when an employee is injured on the job is based on the amount of the employer's payroll. However, due to new hires, raises, terminations, and retirements during the policy period, the employer won't know the actual size of its payroll until the end of the policy period. It is only after the policy period is over that the insurer and the insured are able to determine how much the premium should be.

The insured pays an estimated premium at the beginning of the policy period. At the end of the policy period, typically one year, a premium auditor examines, or audits, the insured's records to determine the final premium. If the final premium exceeds the estimated premium, an additional premium is charged. If the final premium is less than the estimated premium, the insured receives a partial refund.

Because of their direct contact with policyholders, premium auditors also have an opportunity to share their observations with other insurer departments. Auditors can notify underwriters of larger loss exposures than originally contemplated, unacceptable operations, new products, new operations, or financial problems. Premium audit information can also identify marketing opportunities and assist the claim department in adjusting certain types of losses.

---

## Apply Your Knowledge

For each of these actions, identify the insurance function that is most closely associated with it:

Determining the premium for a new customer's personal auto policy

a. Underwriting
b. Risk control
c. Marketing
d. Premium audit

*Feedback: a.* This action is an underwriting function.

Visiting a prospective insured's factory to inspect the fire suppression system

a. Marketing
b. Risk control
c. Premium audit
d. Claims

*Feedback: b.* This action is a risk control function.

Advertising a new policy program for small businesses

a. Risk control
b. Premium audit
c. Marketing
d. Claims

*Feedback:* c. This action is a marketing function.

Visiting an insured's premises after the end of the policy period to examine payroll records for the preceding year

a. Risk control
b. Marketing
c. Claims
d. Premium audit

*Feedback:* d. This action is a premium audit function.

Determining the cause and amount of a policyholder's loss

a. Marketing
b. Underwriting
c. Claims
d. Risk control

*Feedback:* c. This action is a claims function.

---

# PARTIES TO THE INSURANCE TRANSACTION

An insurance transaction occurs when a customer, called the insured or policyholder, purchases insurance either directly from an insurer or through a producer.

Most insurance transactions involve at least two parties: an insured (policyholder) and an insurance company, or insurer. Many other insurance transactions may include a third party, the producer. **Producers** are involved in the sale of insurance products and include sales representatives, agents, and brokers.

Producer

Any of several kinds of insurance personnel who place insurance business with insurers and who represent either insurers or insureds, or both.

## Insured

Property-casualty insurers sell insurance to two broad groups of customers:

- Individuals and families
- Businesses and not-for-profit organizations

Individuals and families purchase personal insurance to insure their nonbusiness exposures. The two major types of personal property-casualty insurance policies are homeowners and personal auto policies.

The property-casualty insurance needs of businesses are generally more complex than those of individuals and families. Businesses and not-for-profit organizations (such as educational, religious, and governmental entities) purchase commercial insurance to insure their loss exposures. Commercial loss exposures are those that affect an organization's operation—for example, damage to business property from loss due to fire or vandalism, work-related injuries to employees, liability for injuries to customers, liability for injuries to others caused by the use of autos, and damage to the insured's own autos.

Because the insured is the party protected by an insurance policy, every insurance policy names at least one insured. However, property and liability policies can also include coverage for parties other than those named insureds. For example, under a homeowners policy, coverage is provided for family members who reside in the home of the individual or couple who are named insureds.

## Insurer

The second party to the insurance transaction is the insurer. Prospective insureds complete insurance applications, which are submitted to one or more insurers. The insurer's staff reviews these applications to determine whether the characteristics of the customer match the insurer's eligibility and selection guidelines. If so, the insurer accepts the exposures of the insured and issues an insurance policy for that customer. If the customer's characteristics do not meet the insurer's guidelines, the insurer will decline to provide coverage, and the customer must then seek insurance coverage with another insurer.

Insurers also collect premiums; pay covered losses; and provide ongoing customer service, such as processing policy changes, providing risk control services, and responding to billing questions.

## Producer

A third possible party to the insurance transaction is the producer. Many insurance policies are sold through a producer.

A producer may be either an insurance agent or an insurance broker. Producers may work independently, or they may be salaried or commissioned employees of an insurer. An independent agent's organization is called an independent agency, and a broker's organization is called a brokerage. An independent agency or a brokerage can consist of one person working alone, or it can include several agents or brokers working with customer service representatives and other specialists. In contrast to an insurance agent or agency, which is the legal representative of one or more insurers, a broker represents the insured in locating insurance coverage and insurers that best meet that customer's needs. See the exhibit "Parties to an Insurance Transaction."

## Parties to an Insurance Transaction

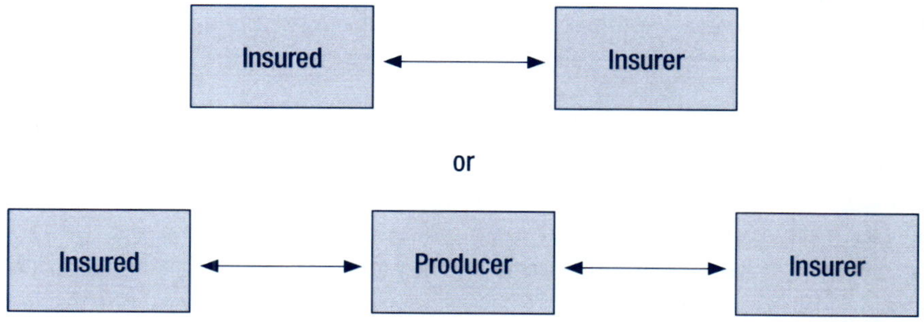


[DA07200]

# INSURANCE MARKETING SYSTEMS

Insurers use many types of marketing systems, also known as distribution channels, designed to meet their particular marketing objectives.

Most insurers use one or more of these marketing systems:

- Independent agency and brokerage marketing system
- Exclusive agency marketing system
- Direct writer marketing system
- Alternative distribution channels

## Independent Agency and Brokerage Marketing System

Producers in the **independent agency and brokerage marketing system** are not employees of any insurer and are usually free to work with as many insurers as they want. They sell insurance products to individuals and businesses and provide policy services, such as analyzing customers' insurance needs, explaining and recommending various coverages and completing the insurance application. Producers may also assist insurers in handling claims made by the producer's customers.

**Independent agency and brokerage marketing system**
An insurance marketing system under which producers (agents or brokers), who are independent contractors, sell insurance, usually as representatives of several unrelated insurers.

A broker is similar to an agent in that the broker also sells insurance products to individuals and businesses and provides policy services. However, the broker represents the prospective insured, while the agent represents the insurer. In practice, despite the technical distinctions between brokers and independent agents, the differences are limited. Brokers and independent agents are intermediaries between insurers and insurance buyers, and both collect premiums from insureds and remit them to insurers. Both are in the business of finding people with insurance needs and selling insurance appropriate to those needs. In fact, some states have eliminated the difference in their licenses and simply refer to them collectively as producers.

Commission
A percentage of the premium that the insurer pays to the agency or producer for new policies sold or existing policies renewed.

Agency expiration list
The record of an insurance agency's present policyholders and the dates their policies expire.

Insurers pay independent agents and brokers a **commission** for each policy sold. Commission rates might vary for new and renewal business and by type of policy.

A distinguishing feature of the independent agency and brokerage system is the ownership of the **expiration list**, commonly referred to as "ownership of expirations." The typical independent agency or brokerage contract specifies that the independent agency or brokerage—not the insurer—owns the list of policyholders and, most importantly, the right to solicit these policyholders for insurance. Policyholders are free to choose another agency or insurer. However, another agency representing the same insurer cannot solicit the policyholder. The exclusive right to solicit policyholders is a valuable asset that can be sold.

An agent or a broker also has the right to sell its expiration list to another independent agent or broker. If the agency or brokerage were to be sold, for example, the buyer would want to keep the previous owner's customers and would need the expiration list to solicit those customers.

## Exclusive Agency Marketing System

Exclusive agency marketing system
An insurance marketing system under which agents contract to sell insurance exclusively for one insurer (or for an associated group of insurers).

The **exclusive agency marketing system** uses independent contractors called exclusive agents, who represent only one insurer or a group of related insurers, possibly under common ownership. Like independent agents, exclusive agents are independent contractors and are not employees of an insurer. In contrast to independent agents, most exclusive agents have contracts that prohibit them from selling insurance for any other insurer.

The insurer often handles many administrative functions for the exclusive agency. These functions include policy issuance, premium collection, and claim processing. Exclusive agents might offer some claim handling services similar to those offered by independent agents and brokers.

Exclusive agents are usually paid commissions, and the commission percentage is sometimes higher for new business than it is for renewal business. Exclusive agents may also receive a bonus for exceeding sales goals. Unlike independent agents, exclusive agents do not own the policy expirations; the insurer does. Therefore, if an exclusive agent does not renew its agency contract with the insurer, the insurer retains control of the policies written by the exclusive agent.

## Direct Writer Marketing System

The **direct writer marketing system** is similar to the exclusive agency system in that the sales representatives used by the insurer are restricted to representing only that insurer or a group of insurers under common ownership and management. However, in contrast to an exclusive agent, a direct writer agent is employed by the insurer and receives a salary, a bonus, commissions, or a combination of the three. See the exhibit "Differences Among Insurance Marketing Systems."

**Direct writer marketing system**
An insurance marketing system that uses sales agents (or sales representatives) who are direct employees of the insurer.

### Differences Among Insurance Marketing Systems

| Type of Marketing System | Contractual Relationship With Insurers | Method of Compensation | Ownership of Expirations | Insurers Represented |
|---|---|---|---|---|
| Independent agency and brokerage marketing system | Independent contractors (not employees of insurer) | Commissions | Producer owns expirations | Usually more than one insurer |
| Exclusive agency marketing system | Independent contractors (not employees of insurer) | Commissions and bonus | Insurer owns expirations | Only one insurer |
| Direct writer marketing system | Employees of insurer | Salary, bonus, commissions, or a combination | Insurer owns expirations | Only the producer's employer |

[DA00027]

Because direct writer agents are employees of the insurers they represent, they do not have any ownership of expirations. Like exclusive agents, agents for direct writers are largely free of responsibility for administrative functions, which are handled by the insurer.

## Alternative Distribution Channels

In addition to the three traditional marketing systems, insurers or producers also use these alternative distribution channels to sell insurance:

- Direct response
- Internet
- Call centers

- Group marketing
- Financial institutions

**Direct response distribution channel**
An insurance distribution channel that markets directly to the customer through such distribution channels as mail, telephone, or the Internet.

The **direct response distribution channel** does not use producers. Although this distribution channel is also called direct mail, customers can contact insurers via the Internet or telephone, not just by mail. Direct response relies heavily on advertising and targeting specific groups of affiliated customers.

The Internet is another alternative distribution channel. The Internet can be used by all parties to the insurance transaction: the insurer, the producer, and the customer. Customers can interact with insurers via Internet-based insurance distributors, also called insurance portals or aggregators. These portals deliver potential customers' contact information to the insurers whose products they offer through their Web sites.

Call centers are also alternative distribution channels. The best-equipped call centers can replicate many of the activities of producers. In addition to making product sales, call center staff respond to general inquiries, handle claim processing, answer billing questions, and process policy endorsements.

Group marketing sells insurance products and services to individuals or businesses that are members in the same organization, profession, or age group. The members could also be affiliated by their similar interests or hobbies.

Insurers and producers can also elect to market their products and services through a financial institution. Marketing arrangements can range from a small insurance agency placing an agent at a desk in a local bank to a large insurer forming a strategic alliance with a national financial holding company to solicit customers.

## Apply Your Knowledge

Identify the type of insurance marketing system being used in each of the following instances:

The agency contract specifies that the agent is an independent contractor but is to represent only the insurer named in the contract.

a. Direct response distribution system
b. Exclusive agency marketing system
c. Direct writer marketing system
d. Independent agency and brokerage marketing system

*Feedback: b.* This is an example of the exclusive agency marketing system.

The insurer uses its own employees to sell insurance.

a. Call center distribution system
b. Direct writer marketing system
c. Independent agency and brokerage marketing system
d. Exclusive agency marketing system

*Feedback: b.* This insurer uses the direct writer marketing system.

In the agency contract, the insurer has granted the agency possession and ownership of expirations.

a. Call center distribution system
b. Group marketing system
c. Independent agency and brokerage marketing system
d. Exclusive agency marketing system

*Feedback: c.* This insurer is using the independent agency and brokerage marketing system.

# PRODUCER FUNCTIONS

Producers perform many important functions, which vary from one producer to another.

Generally, the functions that insurance producers are to perform are specified in the agency or brokerage contract. These functions vary widely from one producer to another and depend on the size of the producer's firm, the types of customers, and the complexity of accounts the producer handles. These are a producer's typical functions:

- Prospecting
- Risk management review
- Sales
- Policy issuance
- Premium collection
- Customer service
- Claim handling

Some producers perform all of these functions, while others perform only some of them.

## Prospecting

Prospecting involves locating persons, businesses, and other entities that might be interested in purchasing the insurance products and services offered by the insurer or company the producer represents. Prospects can be located using one of these methods:

- Referrals from present clients
- Referrals from strategic partners (such as banks, real estate brokers, and so forth)
- Advertising and direct mail
- Interactive Web sites
- Telephone solicitations and cold calls

The producer is typically responsible for his or her own prospecting. However, large agencies and brokerages may have employees who specialize in locating prospective clients.

## Risk Management Review

Another function producers perform is risk management review. Risk management review is the principal method used to determine a prospect's insurance needs. For an individual or a family, the risk management review process can be relatively simple, requiring the completion of an interview or a questionnaire that assists in identifying the prospect's loss exposures and that enables the producer to suggest methods—often insurance-based—for treating them.

Because the loss exposures of a business are more complex, the risk management review process for businesses is also likely to be more complex. A substantial amount of the producer's time is required to develop and analyze loss exposure information for a large firm with diversified operations and/or multiple locations.

## Sales

Selling insurance products and services is one of the most important functions of an insurance producer because sales are essential to sustaining the livelihood of the agency or brokerage. Commission on policy premiums produced is the principal source of income for producers and the agencies or brokerages for which they work. Steps in the sales process include contacting the prospective client, determining the prospect's needs, preparing and presenting a proposal, closing the sale, issuing **binders** if necessary, and providing initial customer service.

Binder

A temporary written or oral agreement to provide insurance coverage until a formal written policy is issued.

## Policy Issuance

Another function that some producers perform is policy issuance. Some producers maintain a supply of an insurer's preprinted policies and forms in their offices and issue them as needed to their customers, while other producers use their own agency management systems to generate computer-issued policies on site. More common is insurers' practice of assembling policies at the producer's request and either mailing them directly to policyholders or sending them to the producer for delivery to the insured.

## Premium Collection

Producers who issue policies might also prepare policy invoices and collect premiums. The **agency bill** process may be used for personal insurance policies, but it is more commonly used with large commercial accounts. For small commercial accounts and the majority of personal insurance, the insured is usually directed to send premium payments to the insurer, bypassing the producer in a procedure known as the **direct bill** process.

**Agency bill**

A payment procedure in which a producer sends premium bills to the insured, collects the premium, and sends the premium to the insurer, less any applicable commission.

**Direct bill**

A payment procedure in which the insurer assumes all responsibility for sending premium bills to the insured, collecting the premium, and sending any commission payable on the premium collected to the producer.

## Customer Service

Most producers are involved in customer service to some degree and offer value-added services and personalized insurance packages to differentiate themselves from their competitors in the marketplace. As another example of customer service, the producer might take a policy change request (such as adding a new car to an auto policy), quote a price for additional coverages, or transfer a customer who has had a loss to the claim department.

Additional customer service functions that producers perform include responding to billing inquiries, performing customer account reviews, and engaging in field underwriting (obtaining loss reports, insurance credit scores, motor vehicle reports, and so forth). Producers must be able to respond to questions about policyholders' existing coverage and additional coverage requirements. Finally, producers are expected to facilitate contact between policyholders and insurer personnel, including premium auditors and loss control representatives.

## Claim Handling

All producers are likely to be involved to some extent in handling claims made by their policyholders. Because the producer is the policyholder's principal contact with the insurer, many insureds naturally call the producer first when a claim occurs.

In some cases, the producer may simply give the policyholder the telephone number of the insurer's claim department and possibly the name of a person to speak with. Alternatively, the producer may obtain some basic information about the claim from the policyholder, relay it to the insurer, and arrange for a claim representative to contact the insured. Frequently, insurers issue their policies with a "claim kit" directing their policyholders in the proper procedures and contacts.

Finally, many producers are authorized by their insurers to adjust some types of claims. Most often, the authorization is limited to small property claims—for example, property losses under $5,000. Less frequently, if they are properly trained to do so, some producers are also authorized to settle small liability claims, such as a claim against an insured for collision damage to another driver's car. A few large agencies or brokerages that employ skilled claim personnel might be authorized to settle large, complex claims. The limitations on the producer's claim handling authority should be specified in the agency contract.

Claim handling by qualified producers offers two major advantages: quicker service to policyholders and lower loss adjustment expenses for the insurer. However, if the producer is not properly trained in how to handle claims, overpayment of claims might offset the savings.

## Apply Your Knowledge

Bob, an insurance agent, recently took several actions. For each of these actions, identify which producer function Bob was performing:

He made several cold calls to dry cleaners, one of his specialties.

a. Sales
b. Customer service
c. Risk management review
d. Prospecting

*Feedback: d.* Making cold calls is a prospecting activity.

One of the cold calls resulted in a visit to a dry cleaner's shop, where Bob interviewed the owner to get information about the shop's loss exposures.

a. Premium collection
b. Risk management review
c. Sales
d. Customer service

*Feedback: b.* Bob's interview with the dry cleaner owner may be sufficient to complete his risk management review of this small business.

Bob prepared a proposal and presented it to the dry cleaner, and the proposal was accepted.

a. Policy issuance
b. Customer service
c. Sales
d. Risk management review

*Feedback:* c. Making a successful proposal would fall under the sales function of Bob's position.

After the dry cleaner's policy was issued, the owner called Bob asking for a certificate of insurance. Bob assured the owner he would provide one, and did so.

a. Customer service
b. Claim handling
c. Policy issuance
d. Sales

*Feedback:* a. Providing the certificate of insurance is one of many customer service activities Bob may perform for this customer.

## SUMMARY

Like many businesses, insurers pursue their goals by segmenting operations into functional areas, or departments. These departments must cooperate to serve the primary function of transferring the financial consequences of loss exposures and to meet other insurer goals. An insurer's key functions are marketing, underwriting, claims, risk control, and premium audit. Each department must interact effectively with other departments for the insurer to achieve its goals.

The insurance transaction involves at least two parties: the insured and the insurer. In some cases, a producer is included as a third party to the insurance transaction. The insured can be either an individual or a family who purchases personal insurance, or a business or not-for-profit organization that purchases commercial insurance. The insurer accepts the loss exposures of the insured according to its selection guidelines. The producer, who can be either an agent or a broker, sells insurance products for one or more insurers.

Insurance marketing systems consist of the independent agency and brokerage marketing system, the exclusive agency marketing system, the direct writer marketing system, and alternative distribution channels. These marketing systems differ by these characteristics of the agents or brokers who use each system: their contractual relationship with the insurers whose policies they sell, their method of compensation, and their ownership of expirations. Alternative distribution channels include direct response, Internet, call centers, group marketing, and financial institutions.

An insurance producer's typical functions vary widely from one producer to another and depend on the size of the producer's firm, the types of customers, and the complexity of accounts the producer handles. Producers typically engage in prospecting, risk management review, and sales activities. In addition, they issue policies, prepare policy invoices, and collect premiums, using either the agency bill or direct bill process. Producers also participate in customer service, usually by providing value-added services and personalized insurance packages. Finally, producers often help insureds with claim handling, either by providing helpful information or settling the insured's claim directly.

Direct Your Learning

# 3

# Underwriting

## Educational Objectives

After learning the content of this assignment, you should be able to:

- Explain why each of the following actions is important to the main purpose of underwriting:
  - Minimizing adverse selection
  - Protecting the insurer's available capacity
- Describe the activities performed in the underwriting process.
- Given the insurance rate and exposure units for a particular insurance policy, calculate the policy premium.
- Explain how insurance rates are developed.
- Explain how an insurer's underwriting results are measured using financial and nonfinancial tools.

## Outline

# Underwriting

# 3

## THE PURPOSE OF UNDERWRITING

Through its underwriting function, an insurer develops books of business and maintains profitability.

The purpose of underwriting is to help an insurer develop and maintain a profitable **book of business**. For underwriting to achieve this purpose, insurers must minimize adverse selection and protect their available capacity.

### Minimizing Adverse Selection

Insurers try to select insureds whose covered losses are not likely to exceed the amount the insurer anticipated when it set the price for a particular coverage. When individuals or businesses with the greatest probability of loss apply for a coverage, a situation known as **adverse selection** occurs.

For example, individuals and businesses owning property in an area prone to coastal storms are generally interested in buying property insurance that includes storm coverages such as wind, rain, hail, and flood. Insurance companies, however, usually do not want to provide property insurance to applicants who expect frequent, severe losses.

Underwriters minimize adverse selection by carefully selecting the applicants whose loss exposures they are willing to insure. By minimizing adverse selection, underwriters reduce the likelihood of insured loss levels that would result in unprofitable business.

### Protecting the Insurer's Capacity

Without adequate **capacity**, an insurer cannot develop and maintain a profitable book of business. An insurer's capacity is limited by regulatory guidelines and often by its own voluntary constraints, which are frequently more conservative than those imposed by regulators.

An insurer's capacity increases as the amount of its **policyholders' surplus** increases. Therefore, if an insurer's underwriting practices generate policy premiums that exceed losses and expenses, the policyholders' surplus will increase, thereby increasing capacity.

**Book of business**

A group of policies with a common characteristic, such as territory or type of coverage, or all policies written by a particular insurer or agency.

**Adverse selection**

In general, the tendency for people with the greatest probability of loss to be the ones most likely to purchase insurance.

**Capacity**

The amount of business an insurer is able to write, usually based on a comparison of the insurer's written premiums to its policyholders' surplus.

**Policyholders' surplus**

Under statutory accounting principles (SAP), an insurer's total admitted assets minus its total liabilities.

# THE UNDERWRITING PROCESS

Whether relying on independent judgment or the guidance of expert systems, underwriters engage in an underwriting decision-making process designed to ensure that, ultimately, insurers are able to reach their business goals.

An underwriting decision regarding acceptability, in addition to other underwriting issues, must be made on every new insurance application submitted to an insurer. Underwriting decisions must also be made on renewal policies as well as on certain policy changes (such as a request to add a driver to an auto policy). Traditionally, an insurance company underwriter has made these decisions. Insurers increasingly use **expert systems**, which help them make better and more consistent underwriting decisions. Expert systems, also known as knowledge-based systems or rules-based systems, are most frequently used in personal lines and small commercial lines insurance, but their ability to handle large commercial accounts is growing.

Expert systems, or knowledge-based systems
Computer software programs that supplement the underwriting decision-making process. These systems ask for the information necessary to make an underwriting decision, ensuring that no information is overlooked.

The underwriting process consists of these activities:

- Gathering the necessary information
- Making the underwriting decision
- Implementing the underwriting decision
- Monitoring the underwriting decision

## Gathering the Necessary Information

To make a decision on new insurance accounts, as well as on certain renewal policies or policy changes, underwriters need adequate information to determine the potential risk that each applicant represents. The application for insurance contains the applicant's responses to questions the insurer has asked and thus provides essential underwriting information. Underwriters can obtain information from various other sources, such as these:

- Producers—In addition to completing and submitting applications, producers might supply information not included on applications or renewals, such as a business's annual report, a preliminary risk control review, or a producer's professional recommendation of an applicant.
- Inspection reports—Many insurers employ risk control representatives, whose duties include physically inspecting the premises, reviewing the operations of insurance applicants, and preparing reports for underwriters.
- Government records—Motor vehicle records (MVRs) are commonly used in underwriting auto insurance. Underwriters can also seek pertinent information in court documents and public records relating to property ownership.
- Financial rating services—Firms such as Dun & Bradstreet (D&B) and Standard & Poor's (S&P) provide data on the credit rating and financial stability of specific businesses. In personal lines, some insurers use insur-

ance scoring, a form of **predictive modeling** that uses a statistical analysis of credit report information to identify the relative likelihood of an insurance loss based on the actual loss experience of individuals with similar financial patterns.

- Claim files—An applicant's loss history is usually provided to an underwriter when an application is submitted to the insurer. However, after a policy has been issued, an insured might file one or more new claims. The claim process generates additional information that is then stored in, and accessible from, the insurer's claim files.
- Applicant's or insured's records—Underwriters can sometimes obtain information from an applicant's or insured's records, such as copies of jewelry appraisals (for valuation purposes) and property bills of sale. For businesses, the annual report, which describes a firm's operations and plans and contains its financial statements (including the balance sheet and income statement), provides much useful underwriting information. Most businesses have Web sites that also can be sources of valuable information.

**Predictive modeling**

A process in which historical data based on behaviors and events are blended with multiple variables and used to construct models of anticipated future outcomes.

## Making the Underwriting Decision

After obtaining all pertinent information, an underwriter evaluates an application to determine the risk posed by the applicant, the underwriting options available, and the appropriate pricing. When an expert system is being used to make underwriting decisions, the underwriting information is entered into a computer program that either assists the underwriter in making a decision or makes the decision independently.

One way an underwriter determines the level of risk posed by an applicant is by analyzing information about the conditions affecting the applicant, called **hazards**, that may increase the chance of loss. Examples of hazards are an inexperienced driver in regard to auto insurance and poor maintenance of fire extinguishers in relation to insurance on a building.

**Hazard**

A condition that increases the frequency or severity of a loss.

To make an underwriting decision, an underwriter must consider whether the hazards presented by the applicant make the level of overall risk desirable or undesirable. In evaluating each application, an underwriter has three options:

- Accept the application without modification
- Reject the application
- Accept the application with modification

An application may be so desirable, or so undesirable, that the underwriter will accept it with no changes or reject it outright. The last option, accepting the application with modification, requires the greatest amount of underwriting expertise.

Generally, the underwriter, producer, and applicant all want the insurance policy to be issued. If the particular coverage requested cannot be provided, the underwriter can often offer alternative terms and conditions that satisfy all parties. Alternatives available to underwriters to make a risk more acceptable include requiring additional risk control measures, modifying the policy provisions, and modifying the premium.

Often a policy can be issued if the applicant agrees to implement additional risk control measures. For example, an underwriter might agree to write property insurance for a particular bookstore, provided the store owner installs and maintains an appropriate fire alarm system.

Deductible

A portion of a covered loss that is not paid by the insurer.

When a producer requests a particular set of policy provisions or insuring terms for an applicant, such as a coverage **deductible** or specific policy form, such provisions or terms are usually contingent on an underwriter's review of the account. For example, if an applicant has had frequent losses of the type to be insured, the underwriter might recommend increasing the deductible, adding certain exclusions to the policy form requested, or using an alternative policy form that provides narrower coverage than the one requested. Each of these modifications reduces the insurer's exposure to loss.

Another way to make an application acceptable is to modify the price charged for the coverage. A producer might have quoted auto insurance using the insurer's "preferred risk" rate, which is a lower rate offered to substantially better-than-average applicants. The underwriter might determine that the applicant does not qualify as a preferred risk but would be acceptable for coverage at standard class prices.

After careful review of hazards, underwriting options, and pricing, the underwriter can then make the best possible decision available for a particular account. Each alternative presented, such as following risk control recommendations or accepting modified coverage, requires the agreement of the applicant and might involve further negotiation. In such situations, the underwriter normally contacts the producer to negotiate the issues with the applicant.

## Implementing the Underwriting Decision

After making an underwriting decision, the underwriter implements the decision. All decisions, whether the application is accepted, rejected, or accepted with modification, are clearly communicated to the producer and to other insurer personnel. If the underwriting decision is made using expert systems and the application is approved, the policy will automatically be issued to the producer and the insured. This approach is typical with routine applications for auto insurance, homeowners insurance, and small commercial accounts. If the decision is not fully automated and is consistent with underwriting guidelines and within the underwriter's authority, the underwriter can approve the application for policy issuance.

Some applications an underwriter wants to approve may exceed the underwriter's authority and require a supervisor's approval. The supervisor might simply approve or reject the underwriter's recommendation or might refer the entire application to a more specialized or experienced underwriter for review. The second underwriter may approve, reject, or modify the first underwriter's recommendation.

## Monitoring the Underwriting Decision

The underwriting process does not end when a policy is issued. The underwriter must continually monitor the results of the initial underwriting decision. Underwriters do this by monitoring claims activity on policies, monitoring the hazards that develop from changes to the policies, and monitoring the overall profitability of the book of business for which each underwriter is responsible.

By monitoring the nature and number of claims that develop, underwriters can evaluate whether additional underwriting action is required. The fact that an insured experiences a serious loss or several losses does not necessarily mean that the underwriter made a bad decision. Conversely, a lack of serious losses does not necessarily mean that the underwriter made a good decision in accepting the account. The occurrence or the nonoccurrence of losses might be a matter of chance.

If serious problems develop with an account, the underwriter might need to take corrective action. Such action can include recommending additional risk control measures, modifying the terms of coverage, canceling coverage (if permitted by regulatory authorities), or marking the policy for nonrenewal at the end of the current policy term.

During the policy term, the policyholder might request one or more coverage changes. The underwriter must carefully consider and implement each request as appropriate. Some changes present no increased hazard, while others might increase the potential for losses. For example, a change of vehicle on an automobile policy from a five-year-old sedan to a five-year-old coupe does not necessarily represent an increased hazard, but it might if at the same time a young driver is added as an additional operator.

Despite the variations in the hazards or loss experience of individual accounts, the entire group of accounts an underwriter handles is expected to meet the profitability goals established for the book of business. Careful monitoring of each account helps the underwriter meet these goals.

Finally, as the policy expiration date approaches, the underwriter might need to repeat the underwriting process before agreeing to renew the policy for another term. Renewal underwriting can generally be accomplished more quickly than new-business underwriting because the insured is already known to the underwriter and more information might be available as claim reports or risk control reports have been added to the file. However, the underwriter must determine whether any changes in the account have occurred and, if so, repeat the underwriting process.

Many insurers do not repeat the entire underwriting process at every renewal for existing small commercial insurance policies and personal insurance policies. Instead, they continue to renew these policies until a particular activity triggers an underwriting review. Claims, requests for coverage changes, or the passage of a certain amount of time might prompt an insurer to repeat the underwriting process. See the exhibit "The Underwriting Process."

**The Underwriting Process**

- Gathering the necessary information
- Making the underwriting decision
- Implementing the underwriting decision
- Monitoring the underwriting decision

[DA00028]

# PREMIUM DETERMINATION

One of the main activities performed by the underwriting department is pricing, or determining the policy premium, an activity commonly called "rating."

An insurance premium is a periodic payment by the insured to the insurer in exchange for insurance coverage. "Periodic" means that the payment must be made at certain time intervals. Each premium payment buys insurance protection for a particular time period, such as one year.

Although the terminology is different, insurance premiums are determined in much the same way as the prices of other products. For example, in many grocery stores, the "unit price" for each item is shown on the shelf. If an eighteen-ounce jar of peanut butter costs $2.34, the unit price is $0.13 per ounce and the final price is $2.34. In this case, one ounce is the unit.

In insurance, the premium (final price) is calculated by multiplying the insurance rate (unit price) by the number of exposure units. Depending on the type of coverage being rated, additional steps may be needed, such as adding charges for optional coverages.

Rate

The price per exposure unit for insurance coverage.

Rate manual

A resource for classifying accounts and developing premiums for given types of insurance; includes necessary rules, factors, and guidelines to apply those rates.

## Insurance Rates

An insurance **rate** is the "unit price" for insurance. Multiplying the rate by the number of exposure units determines the premium. Typically, an insurer has a separate rate in its **rate manual** for each of the rating classifications it uses. An insurer may have hundreds of rating classifications for a particular type of insurance. Rating classifications are based on characteristics of the insured and the loss exposures being insured.

The *ISO Commercial Lines Manual (CLM)* provides classification tables that contain hundreds of classifications of commercial business operations. When calculating the premium for commercial accounts, underwriters typically determine the insured's business operation and then find the appropriate rating classification in the applicable classification table. See the exhibit "Classification Table."

### Classification Table

**51300 Baby Food Mfg. – In glass containers**

Class Code: 51300

Premium Base: Gross Sales

**10100 Bakeries**

Class Code: 10100

Premium Base: Gross Sales

Note: This classification includes baking operations at the same location as the store, if the products baked are sold principally in that store.

**51315 Bakery Plants**

Class Code: 51315

Premium Base: Gross Sales

Note: Risks shall be classified and rated as bakeries, if products baked are sold principally in the insured's own retail store at the same location.

**10111 Barber or Beauty Shop Supplies Distributors**

Class Code: 10111

Premium Base: Gross Sales



## Exposure Units

The fundamental measures of the loss exposures used in insurance rating are referred to as **exposure units**. Insurers use standardized exposure units for rating most types of insurance. For example, in homeowners insurance, exposure units are normally expressed as $1,000 of insured value. In the case of a home insured for $400,000, the number of exposure units is 400. In the case of a home insured for $200,000, the number of exposure units is 200. See the exhibit "Examples of Exposure Units."

**Exposure unit (unit of exposure)**

The unit of measure (for example, area, gross receipts, payroll) used to determine an insurance policy premium.

### Examples of Exposure Units

| Type of Insurance | Typical Exposure Units |
|---|---|
| Auto | Each vehicle |
| Commercial Property | Each $100 of insured value |
| General Liability | Various exposure units are used, depending on the classification. Some examples are:<br>Each $1,000 of gross sales (for example, a restaurant or retail store)<br>Each $1,000 square feet of area (for example, a school)<br>Each $1,000 of payroll (for example, a consulting firm)<br>Each 1,000 admissions (for example, a movie theater) |
| Homeowners | Each $1,000 of insured value |
| Workers Compensation | Each $100 of payroll |

[DA07494]

## Calculation of Premium (Rate x Exposure Units)

After the insurance rate and number of exposure units are known, calculating the premium involves a relatively simple mathematical formula. This type of calculation is similar to that used in pricing many products that consumers purchase.

Consider the pricing structure at a produce stand. For example, assume two peaches are sold at the price (or rate) of $0.40 per peach. The cost is determined by multiplying the rate per peach by the number of peaches:

Rate per unit × Number of units = Price.

$0.40 per peach × 2 peaches = $0.80.

The same formula is used if five pounds of peaches are sold at the produce stand at a price of $0.98 per pound:

Rate per unit × Number of units = Price.

$0.98 per pound × 5 pounds = $4.90.

In both examples, the total cost is composed of a rate ($0.40 or $0.98) for some standard unit of purchase (peach or pound) multiplied by the number of units (two peaches and five pounds, respectively). The choice of standard units is a matter of convenience. For instance, peaches might be priced "per peach" or "by the pound"; gasoline in the United States is usually priced by the gallon, but in many other countries it is priced by the liter.

Underwriters who are calculating insurance premiums follow essentially the same process in determining premiums as is followed in calculating the price of commodities. Based on rates contained in the insurer's rating manuals, the final price of insurance (the premium) is determined by multiplying the rate per unit by the number of exposure units:

Rate per unit × Number of exposure units = Premium.

The formula is the same as before, except that in this instance, the word "premium" is substituted for the word "price." For example, if the insurance rating system shows a rate of $900 per auto to provide collision coverage for one year, this rate is multiplied by the number of autos to arrive at the annual premium. Consider a company with five autos to insure—the computation would be simple:

Rate per unit × Number of exposure units = Premium.

$900 per auto × 5 autos = $4,500.

Many insurance rating units are expressed in dollar amounts, such as "$100 of insured value" or "$1,000 of payroll."

A commercial property policy has a rate of $0.50 per $100 of building insurance, and the building is being insured for $600,000.

Insured value ÷ Unit size = Number of exposure units

$600,000 ÷ $100 = 6,000 units

Rate per unit × Number of exposure units = Premium

$0.50 × 6,000 = $3,000

## Other Factors Affecting Premium Determination

Although a major part of establishing premiums is calculating rate times exposure units, other factors can affect premium determination. Manual or class rates usually serve as a standard for a type of insurance (such as homeowners or commercial auto) and are intended to represent the average risk in a class. However, there are many variations from the average.

Underwriters vary from the manual rate to reflect the reality of actual exposures to loss, the specific characteristics of those exposures, and competitive market influences. Underwriters can use experience or schedule rating plans to reflect the differences between the applicant and the average risk. Underwriters apply experience or scheduled rating credits to "better-than-average" risks and experience or scheduled debits to "worse-than-average" risks. For example, an underwriter might apply a 10 percent premium reduction to a better-than-average risk and a 5 percent premium increase to a worse-than-average risk.

Various other factors can affect final premiums, such as minimum premiums, increased limit factors for liability insurance, additional charges for certain coverage options, good-student discounts, and fire protection systems.

### Apply Your Knowledge

ABC Company is a new business that provides Internet marketing services to commercial clients. ABC is applying for workers compensation insurance for its seven employees who are classified as clerical employees. The manual rate is $0.30 per $100 of payroll. ABC's annual payroll is $500,000.

Calculate the basic premium that would be charged for ABC's seven employees, ignoring any additional rating factors that might apply.

a. $300

b. $3,000

c. $1,500

d. $10,500

*Feedback:* c. Rate × Exposure units = Premium. $0.30 × ($500,000 ÷ $100) = $1,500.

Ratemaking

The process insurers use to calculate insurance rates, which are a premium component.

Actuary

A person who uses mathematical methods to analyze loss data and develop insurance rates.

Insurance rating system

The price per exposure unit determined by adjusting the prospective loss costs for expenses, profits, and contingencies.

Loss costs

The portion of the rate that covers projected claim payments and loss adjusting expenses.

## RATEMAKING

Many insurers have a separate department that is responsible for the development of insurance rates, commonly called ratemaking. In some instances, underwriters may be responsible for ratemaking.

**Ratemaking** is a complex process that requires analysis of both external and internal data. Most insurers employ **actuaries** who perform the analyses, usually as part of a separate actuarial department.

Insurance rates, the basic price of insurance for each unit of exposure, are developed through **insurance rating systems** established by insurers and independent insurance advisory organizations. Typically, insurance rating systems are primarily based on insurers' **loss costs**. Insurance advisory organizations develop loss cost information by using either class or individual rating methodologies to analyze and categorize insureds.

In determining the final rate for a particular loss exposure, an insurer adds an allowance for expenses and profits to the basic rate that has been developed from loss costs. The insurer's underwriting department then determines the final premium by multiplying the final rate by the number of exposure units.

## Insurance Advisory Organizations

**Insurance advisory organizations** work with insurers in developing insurance rating systems. The largest insurance advisory organization is Insurance Services Office, Inc. (ISO), which provides analytical and decision-support products and services to the property-casualty industry. The National Council on Compensation Insurance (NCCI) is an insurance advisory organization that manages a database of workers compensation insurance information, analyzes industry trends, prepares workers compensation rate recommendations, and assists in developing state-specific workers compensation forms and endorsements. Other insurance advisory organizations that operate on a countrywide basis include the American Association of Insurance Services and the Surety and Fidelity Association of America.

Insurance advisory organization

An independent corporation that works with and on behalf of insurers that purchase or subscribe to their services, which include developing prospective loss costs and standard policy forms.

## Insurance Rating Systems

Insurance advisory organizations help develop insurance rating systems by collecting reliable loss data that insurers use in establishing their rates and premiums. Insurance advisory organizations continually collect loss information from many insurers. For example, to assist insurers in determining an appropriate rate to charge for automobile insurance during a certain period, insurance advisory organizations may gather data on insurers' loss costs for automobile accidents involving certain types of vehicles during a particular year.

Insurance rating systems combine loss data from many insurers, an approach based on the **law of large numbers**. Including losses of a large number of exposure units makes the resulting loss data more reliable than an individual insurer's loss data.

Law of large numbers

A mathematical principle stating that as the number of similar but independent exposure units increases, the relative accuracy of predictions about future outcomes (losses) also increases.

Insurance advisory organizations then analyze the loss data to determine the average loss costs per exposure unit used in class rating. See the exhibit "Rate Development Process."

### Loss Costs

Loss data reflect historical loss costs—costs that occurred in the past. Insurers often adjust data on historical loss costs in anticipation of losses that can be expected in the future as a result of inflation or other measurable trends. These **prospective loss costs** indicate the amount of money an insurer can expect to pay for future claims for each exposure unit. However, it is not enough for insurers to collect money only to pay claims. An insurer must also cover its expenses and allow for profits and **contingencies**. Therefore, each insurer uses loss cost information to develop its own set of rates per exposure unit, determining how much to add to basic rates to arrive at the final rate it will charge.

Prospective loss costs

Loss data that are modified by loss development, trending, and credibility processes, but without considerations for profit and expenses.

Contingencies

A provision in an insurance rate for losses that could not be anticipated in the loss data.

Once determined, rates are published in an insurer's rating manual or stored in the insurer's rating system. These rates are also filed with the state

### Rate Development Process

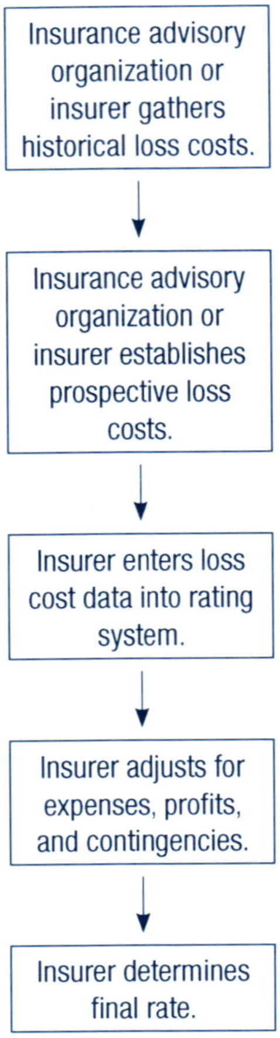


Note: After the final rate is determined, the insurer multiplies it by the number of exposure units to determine the final premium.

[DA00467]

insurance department where required. In many cases, the state insurance department might also reject, modify, or approve the rates that will be used.

## Class Rating

Class rating

A rating approach that uses rates reflecting the average probability of loss for businesses within large groups of similar risks; the predominant method used for rating commercial properties.

Insurers develop loss costs for many different lines (or types) of business and many different groups or classes of insureds within those lines. Many kinds of insurance are priced using **class rating**. All members of a class are charged the same rate for insurance, although their premiums will be different if they have different numbers of exposure units. For example, a homeowner with a $400,000 home will pay more for homeowners insurance than a homeowner with a $200,000 home.

The basic premise of an insurance classification and rating system is that insureds with similar characteristics have similar potential loss frequency and severity. Even though wide variation in actual losses may occur from one insured to the next, aggregate losses among all members of the class should be predictably different from the losses of all members of another class who have different characteristics. For example, an employer will pay more for workers compensation insurance for a construction worker than for a clerical worker because construction workers as a class are more likely to become injured or disabled on the job than clerical workers as a class.

While no two risks are identical, grouping them enables an insurer to take advantage of pooling. The groupings or classes should be big enough to reflect the law of large numbers but small enough that all members share characteristics related to frequency and severity of loss.

## Individual Rating

When insureds cannot be readily assigned to the same class, the insured loss exposure is rated individually. For example, an **individual rate, or specific rate**, might be developed for fire insurance on a large, unique factory building. The specific building is inspected by an underwriting professional using a point system that adds or subtracts points for such things as type of construction (masonry, wood, and so on), number and type of fire extinguishers, nature of the occupancy, capabilities of the local fire department, and the supply of water available at nearby hydrants. The number of points determines an insurance rate for that particular building. The rate is applied "per $100 of insurance" to determine the premium for fire insurance.

Individual rate, or specific rate

A type of insurance rate that reflects the unique characteristics of an insured or the insured's property.

Sometimes it is necessary to insure an exposure for which there is no established premium-determining system. In such cases, the underwriter has to rely heavily on his or her judgment, a practice that is referred to as **judgment rating**. Judgment rating is a type of individual rating.

Judgment rating

Rating used by underwriters to rate one-of-a-kind risks.

Judgment rating does not mean that an underwriter arbitrarily sets a rate for a particular exposure. The underwriter usually has experience with insurance covering comparable exposures and a resulting sense of what premium amount would be appropriate. For example, successful experience in insuring cross-country rail shipments of coal and iron ore might help an underwriter to decide the premium to charge for insuring the shipment of some other bulk cargo.

## Final Rate and Premium Determination

**Final rates** result from prospective loss costs that move through the rating system and become adjusted for expenses, profits, and contingencies. Insurance rating systems assist insurers in determining rates based on past and expected future losses. The rating systems also account for other factors that affect insurers' final rate determination.

Final rate

The price per exposure unit determined by adjusting the prospective loss costs for expenses, profits, and contingencies.

To conduct business, insurers pay not only loss costs but also other expenses, such as underwriting and loss adjustment expenses, and plan for profits and contingencies. To set the final rates, they charge insureds for particular loss exposures. Individual insurers, therefore, add an allowance for factors such as expenses, profits, and contingencies to the basic insurance rates developed through insurance rating systems.

After the final rate has been calculated, it is multiplied by the number of exposure units to determine the final insurance premium.

# MEASURING UNDERWRITING RESULTS

An insurer's underwriting results provide a key indicator of its level of profitability. Without a clear understanding of underwriting performance, insurers may not recognize and effectively respond to positive and negative conditions in their business. Insurers typically track their underwriting results through the use of both financial and nonfinancial tools.

The financial tools that insurers use to measure underwriting results include the loss ratio, expense ratio, and combined ratio. Nonfinancial tools may vary according to the line of insurance, but typically include measurements of product mix, pricing, retention ratio, success ratio, and customer service.

## Financial Tools

Loss ratio

A ratio that measures losses and loss adjustment expenses against earned premiums and that reflects the percentage of premiums being consumed by losses.

Earned premiums

The portion of written premiums that corresponds to coverage that has already been provided.

Incurred losses

The sum of the paid losses and loss and loss adjustment expense reserves.

Loss adjustment expense (LAE)

The expense that an insurer incurs to investigate, defend, and settle claims according to the terms specified in the insurance policy.

The financial tools that insurers use to measure results include calculations and ratios. Three ratios are typically used to assess an insurer's underwriting results.

$$\text{Loss ratio} = \frac{\text{Incurred losses (including loss adjustment expenses)}}{\text{Earned premiums}}$$

$$\text{Expense ratio} = \frac{\text{Underwriting expenses}}{\text{Written premiums}}$$

$$\text{Combined ratio} = \text{Loss ratio} + \text{Expense ratio}$$

The **loss ratio**, commonly expressed as a percentage, indicates what portion of the insurer's **earned premiums** goes to **incurred losses**, including **loss adjustment expense (LAE)**. This ratio provides an insurer with a tool to assess how closely actual loss experience compares to expected loss experience. For example, at the beginning of the year, management might have decided that an 85 percent loss ratio is the coming year's target. The loss ratio is then continuously monitored to determine whether it is at or below 85 percent and whether it meets management's expectations. An insurer's loss ratio gives a general indication of the quality of business the insurer writes and might also provide insight into the adequacy of the insurer's rates.

The **expense ratio**, commonly expressed as a percentage, indicates what portion of an insurer's **written premiums** is being used to pay the company's **underwriting expenses**. In effect, the expense ratio is a tool to measure an insurer's general cost of producing business as a proportion of the premiums it has written. Comparing the expense ratios for successive time periods indicates overall expense trends, with an increasing expense ratio potentially highlighting the need for more effective expense controls.

The **combined ratio** measures an insurer's underwriting profit. It is called the combined ratio because it combines the loss ratio and the expense ratio. If total losses and expenses exceed the premium, the combined ratio will be more than 100 percent, signifying an **underwriting loss**. A combined ratio less than 100 percent signifies an **underwriting profit**. See the exhibit "Example of Application of Financial Tools to Determine Underwriting Result."

### Example of Application of Financial Tools to Determine Underwriting Result

Barnley Insurance Company had $5,435,546,832 in written premiums and $5,386,256,843 in earned premiums for the current year. The incurred losses (including LAE) were $4,222,825,365, and the underwriting expenses were $1,077,251,369.

$$\text{Loss ratio} = \frac{\$4{,}222{,}825{,}365}{\$5{,}386{,}256{,}843} = 0.78 = 78\%$$

$$\text{Expense ratio} = \frac{\$1{,}077{,}251{,}369}{\$5{,}435{,}546{,}832} = 0.20 = 20\%$$

$$\text{Combined ratio} = 0.78\ (78\%) + 0.20\ (20\%) = 0.98 = 98\%$$

Barnley's combined ratio is 98 percent for the current year. This result represents a small underwriting profit.

[DA07517]

**Expense ratio**
An insurer's incurred underwriting expenses for a given period divided by its written premiums for the same period.

**Written premiums**
The total premium on all policies written (put into effect) during a particular period.

**Underwriting expenses**
Costs incurred by an insurer for operations, taxes, fees, and the acquisition of new policies.

**Combined ratio**
A profitability ratio that indicates whether an insurer has made an underwriting loss or gain.

**Underwriting loss**
An insurer's loss incurred when losses and expenses for a given period are greater than its premium earned for the same period.

**Underwriting profit**
Income an insurer earns from premiums paid by policyholders minus incurred losses and underwriting expenses.

## Nonfinancial Tools

An insurer's success depends on the ability of the underwriting function to achieve the insurer's profitability goals over the long term. There are many factors that determine how effectively the underwriting function has been performing. Evaluating underwriting effectiveness is accomplished, in part, through the use of nonfinancial tools.

Nonfinancial tools link an organization's business strategy and its **outputs** to its performance. In a general business context, two common examples of non-

**Output**
Any product or service that results from a work process.

financial tools to measure performance are the quality of customer service and the volume of goods produced. In the insurance industry, nonfinancial tools used to assess an insurer's underwriting results often include these:

- Product mix
- Pricing
- Retention ratio
- Success ratio
- Customer service

Some of these tools apply only to commercial lines or personal lines, while others apply to both. Methods of applying these nonfinancial tools include computer systems and underwriting audits. An insurer's senior managers and its underwriters typically work together to develop nonfinancial goals and the tools to measure them.

## Product Mix

Measuring product mix is a tool used to evaluate the underwriting function's contribution to an insurer's profitable book of business. Building a profitable book of business requires that underwriters have a thorough knowledge of the insurer's business goals, including the types of products it prefers to write and the "appetite" the insurer has for certain types of risk.

For example, one insurer may have a preference for writing automobile insurance in a particular state. Although the insurer may have the capacity to write homeowners insurance, it may prefer not to do so for business reasons. Another insurer, operating in the same state, could have exactly the opposite preferences. Underwriters need to consider how well the business they choose to accept (or price attractively) aligns with their employers' business strategies.

## Pricing

Insurers usually set pricing standards as a nonfinancial measure. Pricing standards enable insurers to determine levels of premium adequacy by comparing the premiums actually charged to the standards.

For example, in commercial insurance, where rates are often not regulated, underwriters typically modify rates for each account to reflect the specific features of that account. The insurer's pricing standards indicate the extent to which these modifications depart from the insurer's standard pricing model.

If one or more underwriters usually apply excessive premium credits to accounts to obtain new business or to retain it on renewal, an underwriting audit might indicate that profitability is being sacrificed in return for short-term growth.

## *Apply Your Knowledge*

Barnley Insurance Company's combined ratio increased from 98 percent to 103 percent. What does this indicate about Barnley's profitability?

a. Barnley went from an underwriting profit to an underwriting loss.

b. Barnley went from an underwriting loss to an underwriting profit.

c. Barnley's underwriting profit increased somewhat.

d. Barnley's underwriting loss decreased somewhat.

*Feedback: a.* Barnley went from an underwriting profit to an underwriting loss. A combined ratio of less than 100 percent represents an underwriting profit. Therefore, Barnley went from an underwriting profit, with a combined ratio of 98 percent, to an underwriting loss with a combined ratio of 103 percent.

## Retention Ratio

The longer an insurer retains a policy in its book of business, the more profitable that policy becomes as measured by the expense ratio. Although there may be reasons why an insurer does not want to renew a policy, such as a high loss ratio, most insurers prefer to acquire and retain profitable accounts. The **retention ratio** measures an insurer's success in maintaining its book of business.

Retention ratio
The percentage of insurance policies renewed.

Too low a retention ratio might indicate deficiencies in the insurer's operations, such as poor service to customers or producers, noncompetitive pricing, or unfavorable claim service. This nonfinancial measure requires careful monitoring of renewal negotiations, the competitive environment, and any industry trends that can affect retention.

## Success Ratio

Underwriters often have dual responsibilities. In addition to their responsibilities for underwriting their insurer's book of business, they are responsible for meeting new business sales goals. A **success ratio**, sometimes called a "hit ratio," is a nonfinancial measure used to determine how well the insurer and the underwriting function are meeting the sales goals.

Success ratio
The ratio of insurance policies written to those that have been quoted to applicants for insurance.

Various factors typically lead to either a high or low success ratio. See the exhibit "Success Ratio Factors."

## Customer Service

Insurers use various tools to measure the service they provide to producers, who typically evaluate insurers on service criteria. Insurers also measure the service they provide directly to their insureds.

## Success Ratio Factors

| Factors Leading to High Success Ratio | Factors Leading to Low Success Ratio |
|---|---|
| • Easing of competition | • Increasing competition |
| • Lower rates than other insurers' | • Higher rates than other insurers' |
| • Broader coverage than other insurers' | • More restrictive coverage than other insurers' |
| • Underwriters have the skills to develop relationships with producers and customers | • Underwriters lack the skills to develop relationships with producers and customers |
| • Relaxed underwriting criteria | • Strict underwriting criteria |
| • Good service | • Poor service |

[DA07519]

Examples of areas where standards are set and performance is measured include response time on issuing quotes, turnaround time on applications received, average number of errors per policy issued, response time on inquiries, and number of referrals for potential new business. The performance of a region, an office, or an individual underwriter can be measured and compared against the company standards. See the exhibit "Example of Measuring Customer Service."

## Example of Measuring Customer Service

| Category | Minimum Acceptable Standard |
|---|---|
| 1. Quotations | Three working days |
| 2. New policies | Three working days |
| 3. Replies to correspondence | Two working days |
| 4. Cancellations, endorsements, certificates | Five working days |
| 5. Direct cancellation notices | Same-day service |
| 6. Renewals | No later than ten days before expiration |

[DA00035]

# SUMMARY

The purpose of underwriting is to help insurance companies develop and maintain a profitable book of business. Adverse selection and capacity inadequacies must be minimized for underwriting to achieve this purpose.

The underwriting process comprises a series of activities that underwriters perform—often with the assistance of expert systems—that help underwriters make better and more consistent decisions. The steps in the underwriting process include gathering the necessary information, making the underwriting decision, implementing the decision, and monitoring the decision.

Insurers calculate premium by determining the insured's rate classification from a rate manual and multiplying the rate by the number of exposure units. Exposure units are based on the type of coverage and, for commercial insureds, the type of business. Various factors can either increase or decrease the standard rate for a particular insured.

Insurers and independent insurance advisory organizations develop insurance rates through insurance rating systems. Insurance advisory organizations gather historical loss costs from insurers to develop prospective loss costs. Some kinds of insurance are class rated by grouping insureds with similar characteristics into the same rating class to capture potential loss frequency and severity of the group. When an insured cannot be readily assigned to the same class, the insured loss exposure is rated individually.

Insurers add their allowance for their expenses, profits, and contingencies to the basic rate to arrive at the final rate they charge insureds for a particular loss exposure. After the final rate has been calculated, it is multiplied by the number of exposure units to determine the final insurance premium.

Underwriting results are a key indicator of an insurer's profitability; therefore, it is important for insurers to measure underwriting performance. Various factors contribute to the effectiveness of underwriting, and insurers use both financial and nonfinancial tools to measure their underwriting results. Financial tools include these three ratios: loss ratio, expense ratio, and combined ratio. Nonfinancial tools typically measure the product mix, pricing, retention, success of converting prospects to accounts, and customer service.

# Direct Your Learning

# 4

## Claims

### Educational Objectives

After learning the content of this assignment, you should be able to:

- Explain how an insurer's claim function achieves each of its primary goals:
  - Keeping the insurer's promise
  - Supporting the insurer's profit goal
- Identify the activities performed in the claim handling process and the purpose of each.
- Define the role of each of the following in the claim handling process:
  - Claim managers
  - Supervisors
  - Claim representatives
  - Technical specialists
  - Customer service representatives
  - Producers
- Explain how an insurer's claim results are measured using financial and nonfinancial tools.

### Outline

# Claims

# 4

## GOALS OF THE CLAIM FUNCTION

The goals of the claim department include keeping the insurer's promise made in the policy and supporting the insurer's profit goal.

People purchase property-casualty insurance policies to protect against financial losses. When policyholders make claims under their insurance policies, the insurer is called on to honor the promise made in the policy—namely, to indemnify the policyholder for financial losses. This does not imply that the insurer should or will pay every claim that is presented; rather, it implies that the insurer's claim department will conduct a good-faith investigation of a claim and pay only legitimate claims that are covered by the policy.

An insurer's senior management establishes the goals for the claim function. In doing so, managers must equally consider the needs of the insurance customer (the policyholder) and the needs of the insurer. The claim function typically has two primary goals:

- Keeping the insurer's promise
- Supporting the insurer's profit goal

### Keeping the Insurer's Promise

The first goal of the claim function is to satisfy the insurer's obligations to the policyholder as set forth in the insurance contract. In a property insurance policy, the insurer's promise is to pay for direct physical loss to covered property by a covered cause of loss. In a liability insurance policy, the insurer's promise is to pay on behalf of the insured any damages for which the insured is legally liable because of bodily injury, property damage, or other specified types of injury caused by an accident, up to the applicable limit of insurance. The insurer also agrees to defend the insured against claims or suits seeking damages covered by the policy.

The insurer fulfills its promise by providing fair, prompt, and equitable service to the policyholder either directly, when the loss involves a **first-party claim** made by the policyholder against the insurer, or indirectly, when the loss involves a **third-party claim** made against the policyholder by someone to whom the policyholder may be liable. See the exhibit "First-Party Insurance and Third-Party Insurance."

**First-party claim**

A demand by an insured person or organization seeking to recover from its insurer for a loss that its insurance policy may cover.

**Third-party claim**

A demand against an insured by a person or organization other than the insured or the insurer, seeking to recover damages that may be payable by the insured's liability insurance.

**First-Party Insurance and Third-Party Insurance**

Insurance coverage is often referred to as either first-party insurance or third-party insurance.

Property insurance is considered first-party insurance because the insurer makes payment for covered losses directly to the insured. Liability insurance is considered third-party insurance because the insurer makes payments on behalf of the insured (first party) to a claimant (third party) who is injured or whose property is damaged by the insured.

[DA00038]

Claimant

A party that makes a claim and that can be either a first-party claimant or a third-party claimant.

Claim representative

A person responsible for investigating, evaluating, and settling claims.

The insurance contract is marketed not only as a financial mechanism to restore policyholders and other **claimants** to a pre-loss state, but also as a way for policyholders to achieve peace of mind. For a claimant, a loss occurrence and the consequences are not routine and can be overwhelming. A **claim representative** should handle claims in a way that promotes peace of mind for the policyholder who has suffered a loss and that quickly restores a claimant to his or her pre-loss condition.

## Supporting the Insurer's Profit Goal

The second goal of the claim function is to support the insurer's profit goal. Achieving this goal is generally the responsibility of the marketing and underwriting departments; however, the claim function serves a role in generating underwriting profit by controlling expenses and paying only legitimate claims.

By managing all claim function expenses, setting appropriate spending policies, and using appropriately priced providers and services, claim managers can help maintain an insurer's underwriting profit. Similarly, claim staff can avoid overspending on costs of handling claims, claim operations, or other expenses. Finally, by ensuring fair claim settlement, claim representatives prevent any unnecessary increase in the cost of insurance and subsequent reduction in the insurer's underwriting profit.

Policyholders and other claimants are likely to accept an insurer's settlement offer if they believe they are receiving fair treatment. Parties who believe they have been treated unfairly may seek to settle their differences with the insurer by filing lawsuits. Litigation erodes goodwill between the parties and generates increased claim expenses, reducing the insurer's profitability. Additionally, dissatisfied policyholders or claimants may complain to their state insurance department, and, if the state regulatory authorities find fault, an insurer may be subjected to regulatory oversight or penalties. Costs associated with regulatory action can further erode an insurer's profits.

An insurer's success in achieving its profit goal is reflected in its reputation for providing the service promised. A reputation for resisting legitimate claims can undermine the effectiveness of an insurer's advertising. Consequently, the two goals of the claim function work together in support of a profitable insurance operation.

# THE CLAIM HANDLING PROCESS

The claim handling process manages all claims effectively, regardless of the severity or complexity of the loss.

Insurers refer to **claim handling** by various names, some of which are used in specific instances; for example, in property claims, the term "loss adjusting" is often used instead of claim handling. Terms may include claim adjusting, loss adjusting, claim processing, and claim examining; but all refer to the same claim function: complying with the contractual promise made in the insurance policy to satisfy the insurer's obligation to the policyholder.

Claim handling
The insurer function that processes demands for claim payments.

The claim handling process is made up of six activities:

- Acknowledging a claim and assigning it to a claim representative
- Identifying the policy
- Contacting the insured or the insured's representative
- Investigating and documenting the claim
- Determining cause of loss and loss amount
- Concluding the claim

These activities are not sequential, but instead can begin and end at any point in the process and can overlap. Depending on the severity and complexity of the loss, claim handling can be a quick process, completed within hours or days after submission of a claim report, or it can extend over many months.

## Acknowledging a Claim and Assigning It to a Claim Representative

The first claim handling activity an insurer performs is acknowledging receipt of the claim and assigning it to a claim representative. When a loss occurs, the policyholder or the insured reports the loss to the producer, who submits it to the insurer, or the policyholder or insured may report the loss directly to the insurer. In many instances, the policyholder and insured are the same.

The insurer acknowledges receipt of the claim by taking the loss information and creating a claim file. A claim representative is assigned to handle the loss. The claim representative may be a member of the insurer's claim department staff, such as a telephone or field claim representative, or may work for an independent adjusting firm (a business that contracts with insurers to handle claims).

## Identifying the Policy

The claim representative identifies the insurance policy under which the claim is filed and checks it to determine whether it applies to the loss, the coverages that might apply, and the amount of coverage. In addition, the claim representative usually establishes **loss reserves**. However, some claims are concluded immediately without establishing reserves.

Loss reserve

An estimate of the amount of money the insurer expects to pay in the future for losses that have already occurred and been reported, but are not yet settled.

In some cases, claim files are established as "record only," when the insured wants the insurer to have a record of the incident but is not making a claim under the policy. For example, Adam's auto is struck by another vehicle and sustains minor damage. Adam wants to collect damages directly from the insurer of the car that struck his auto. Therefore, Adam reports the accident to his insurer as a record-only claim. By filing the record-only claim, Adam has preserved his right to pursue the claim with his insurer, if his efforts to collect from the other driver's insurer fail. Some insurers will set up a minimum reserve on record-only files; others will not.

## Contacting the Insured or the Insured's Representative

In most cases, the claim representative contacts the insured or the insured's representative soon after establishing reserves. The claim representative may schedule a time to meet with the insured or a party representing the insured as part of the initial contact and verification of coverage.

## Investigating and Documenting the Claim

Investigating and documenting the claim are ongoing activities the claim representative performs to create a complete **claim file**. Claim representatives commonly conduct many investigations, such as insured/witness investigations, claimant investigations, accident scene investigations, and medical investigations. They may consult numerous experts as a part of these investigations. See the exhibit "Experts Consulted in Claims."

Claim file

A paper or an electronic file that contains information for a loss.

In conjunction with their investigations, claim representatives also investigate **subrogation** possibilities to determine whether the insurer can recover any payments it has made from a third party that is legally responsible for the loss.

Subrogation

The process by which an insurer can, after it has paid a loss under the policy, recover the amount paid from any party (other than the insured) who caused the loss or is otherwise legally liable for the loss.

Claim representatives document claims based on the type of loss. For example, in addition to the file status notes, a bodily injury liability claim might include recorded statements of witnesses, copies of medical bills, a physician's diagnosis, and a diagram of the accident scene; in contrast, a broken windshield claim might include only an estimate for the glass replacement with the claim representative's file status notes. Many insurers have claim handling

### Experts Consulted in Claims

| Experts Consulted in Property Claims | Experts Consulted in Liability Claims |
|---|---|
| • Origin and cause experts | • Accident reconstruction specialists |
| • Private investigators | • Accountants |
| • Accountants | • Lawyers |
| • Restoration specialists | • Private investigators |
| • Salvors | • Medical experts |
| • Lawyers | • SIUs |
| • Professionals needed to rebuild | |
| • Appraisers | |
| • Special investigation units (SIUs) | |

[DA00040]

guidelines for documenting each type of claim. Documenting a claim can involve these activities:

- Gathering records
- Photographing or taking video recordings of a loss scene
- Drawing diagrams of damaged areas or accident scenes
- Reviewing the loss notice and financial records or examining inventory to determine the scope of loss
- Taking statements of the involved parties and witnesses
- Obtaining medical records

## Determining Cause of Loss and Loss Amount

The claim representative then uses the results of the investigations and the claim documentation to determine the cause of loss and loss amount. The claim representative compares the information from the loss investigation to the terms of the policy to determine whether the policy covers the cause of loss. If so, the claim representative determines the amount of the loss.

## Concluding the Claim

Once the cause of loss and the loss amount have been determined, the claim can be concluded. The claim representative prepares a loss statement and proceeds to settle the claim. Covered claims are settled with the policyholder or claimant or a representative through negotiation or alternative means of resolution, and the claim representative issues appropriate payments. Claims not covered by the policy are denied. Finally, the claim representative completes closing reports to properly document the claim. These reports enable insurers to track loss payments and claim handling practices, and they complete the documentation if a claim is later litigated.

# ROLES OF CLAIM PERSONNEL

Claim personnel have many roles in effectively performing the claim handling process.

Insurers, producers, and independent adjusting firms and other claim organizations employ claim personnel to fulfill the contractual promise that insurers make to their insureds in insurance policies. Claim department structures and the job titles used to describe claim personnel vary among different types of organizations; however, claim personnel perform basically the same roles despite these differences. The various roles of claim personnel are discussed here using these common job titles:

- Claim manager
- Supervisor
- Claim representative
- Technical specialist
- Customer service representative
- Producer

## Claim Managers

A claim manager directs and supervises the activities of some portion of an insurer's claim department. A claim department may have multiple levels of claim managers. An insurer's management team may include a claim vice president who supervises one or more assistant vice presidents. Assistant vice presidents may be assigned to specific types of insurance, such as workers compensation or auto insurance. Managers at the middle-management level, who may report to assistant vice presidents, usually have the title of claim manager.

An insurance agency or brokerage may have multiple levels of claim managers or none, depending on the volume of business the firm handles. A small firm may have a single general manager who also supervises the claim function.

Some claim departments are divided into sub-departments, each with its own manager. For example, separate managers might oversee property losses, liability losses, workers compensation losses, subrogation, fraud investigation, appraisal, and legal work. Each claim manager may have these responsibilities that affect the claim process:

- Setting goals—Managers set department goals related to claim handling, such as concluding claims that are ready for settlement, managing the cost of each claim, and recovering subrogation amounts.
- Developing staff members' skills—Managers encourage employees to develop their professional skills through training in areas such as improved decision making, claim handling efficiency, and other insurance-related topics.
- Monitoring workloads—Managers monitor workloads to ensure that each claim representative is assigned a manageable number of claim files.
- Monitoring losses and expenses—Managers monitor losses and expenses to identify trends that may indicate the need for additional or specialized training, improvements in claim handling practices, or additional staff.
- Establishing claim procedures and ensuring compliance—Managers establish procedures to ensure that claims are handled promptly and efficiently, in compliance with the organization's guidelines and with state insurance regulations.

## Supervisors

Claim supervisors support the claim management functions of the managers to whom they report. In some organizations, claim departments are divided into units by line of business, such as auto or property, or by geographic location, such as state or designated territories. Each unit has a supervisor who directs its daily activities. Below the supervisor level, reporting relationships vary greatly depending on the structure of the organization.

Supervisors periodically monitor claim files to ensure consistent and accurate claim handling. Claim file reviews help supervisors evaluate claim representatives' performance, develop strategies for solving problems, and determine staff training needs. A supervisor might review each claim file, select only those files that meet specific criteria (such as those with reserves that exceed a certain amount), or examine a random sample of files. Some organizations employ quality control staff to review claim files rather than assign the duty to supervisors.

Claim supervisors usually have technical expertise and often train claim representatives who report to them; for example, they may use informal training meetings to update staff on medical and legal developments that affect claims or on other claim issues. They may also encourage staff members to pursue continuing professional education.

# Claim Representatives

Organizations may employ different types of claim representatives, including telephone claim representatives, field claim representatives, and specialized claim representatives.

## Telephone Claim Representatives

Telephone claim representative, or inside claim representative

An insurer employee who handles claims that can be settled by phone, mail, or e-mail from inside the insurer's office.

**Telephone claim representatives, or inside claim representatives,** handle claims from the organization's office. They investigate claims and evaluate loss amounts based on telephone interviews and correspondence. If additional information or expertise is needed to thoroughly investigate a loss, they may ask field claim representatives for assistance.

Telephone claim representatives can handle small, uncomplicated claims or larger, more complex claims, as determined by claim department procedures and the types of insurance policies the insurer writes. Some organizations use telephone claim representatives to handle nearly every claim.

## Field Claim Representatives

Field claim representative (outside claim representative)

An insurer's employee who handles claims that are best handled in person; much of the field claim representative's time is spent visiting the scene of a loss; interviewing witnesses; investigating damage; and meeting with insureds, claimants, lawyers, and other persons involved in the claim.

Claim representatives who work outside the organization's office are called **field claim representatives.** They generally handle claims that require investigating the scene of a loss; resolving complex investigative issues; or meeting with insureds, claimants, lawyers, and others involved in the claim. Field claim representatives inspect damaged property and work closely with damage appraisers. They often prepare damage estimates, obtain photos and diagrams of accident locations, and negotiate settlements with claimants or their representatives.

An insurer's claim staff may not always be sufficient to complete its claim handling activities. In such cases, additional claim representatives are available through independent adjusting firms. An insurer may contract with these firms when it needs expertise in handling a specific type of claim, when losses have occurred in an area where the insurer has no assigned claim representatives, or when the insurer's claim staff is insufficient to handle current caseloads.

## Specialized Claim Representatives

Depending on the size of a claim organization, claim representatives may specialize in a particular type of claim. The increasing complexities in the claim handling environment often require such specialization. A claim representative who specializes by line of business (such as auto, homeowners, or workers compensation) or state can focus on developing expertise only in the laws and regulations relating to the specialty or state, rather than developing a broader range of knowledge.

For example, a damage appraiser is a field claim representative who specializes in auto physical damage appraisals. An insured with a damaged, but still drivable, auto can take it to a drive-in claim center, where a damage appraiser estimates the cost to repair the vehicle. Damage appraisers prepare their estimates using computer software or **crash manuals**, which may be automated. Based on the estimate, the damage appraiser may immediately issue a check to the insured. The insured can then choose where to have the car repaired. Alternatively, the insured may give the appraiser a damage estimate from a repair facility, and if the appraiser agrees with the estimate, he or she issues the insured a check for the estimate amount.

Crash manual, or estimating guide

A book that describes procedures for estimating the cost to repair damage to vehicles and that lists auto part prices and typical labor times to repair or replace the part.

Field claim representatives may also specialize in heavy construction or pollution liability claims. Because of their expertise, these specialists can often suggest ways to reduce damage amounts. For example, a pollution liability specialist might know whom to contact to quickly contain a pollutant spill and reduce the resulting damage.

Some claim representatives specialize in handling catastrophe claims. Catastrophe claim specialists are trained to handle disasters (such as floods, hurricanes, tornadoes, and earthquakes) that result in multiple losses. Catastrophe claim specialists may travel to the site of a catastrophe, such as a hurricane, and remain there until all claims have been investigated.

## Technical Specialists

Technical specialists assist insurers in determining liability and damages relating to claims. For example, they can help determine who is at fault in an accident and, thus, whether a claim should be paid. Technical specialists may work for a claim organization, such as an independent adjusting firm or a **third-party administrator**, or for a vendor that provides related services. Technical specialists include these:

Third-party administrator (TPA)

An organization that provides administrative services associated with risk financing and insurance.

- Origin and cause experts
- Material damage appraisers
- Reconstruction experts
- Medical consultants
- Rehabilitation nurses

Origin and cause experts investigate fire losses to determine where and how a fire began. Claim personnel often consult these specialists for fires of suspicious origin or when they believe that subrogation possibilities exist.

Material damage appraisers inspect damage to autos and other types of property to determine whether the property is repairable or is a **total loss**. If the property can be repaired, the appraiser estimates the repair costs and negotiates the repair price with the insured's selected repair facility. If the property is a total loss, the appraiser helps the claim representative determine the value of the property and helps locate a buyer for any salvage.

Total loss

A loss that exists when the cost to repair a damaged vehicle (or other property) equals or exceeds the value of the vehicle.

Reconstruction experts specialize in reconstructing the events surrounding automobile accidents. They can describe how an accident occurred and can provide legal testimony as to the vehicles' speeds, braking distances, and what the drivers involved could see before the impact.

Medical consultants and rehabilitation nurses are technical specialists who help claim personnel assess the medical requirements in injury claims. Medical consultants arrange independent medical examinations (IMEs) for injured insureds and claimants and request second opinions from physicians for treatments or surgical procedures. Medical consultants also review medical reports and audit bills from physicians and other medical providers to determine whether the treatment being provided follows the physician's treatment instructions. Rehabilitation nurses help claim representatives assess whether or to what extent rehabilitation is possible for a claimant.

In the field of medical consulting, specialized computer software offers another technical resource for handling claims. For example, medical evaluation software uses artificial intelligence to help claim representatives analyze appropriate medical services.

## Customer Service Representatives

The customer service representative (CSR) is often the insured's or claimant's first contact with the insurer and with the claim handling process. When an insured or a claimant reports a loss directly to the insurer, a CSR generally records the loss information. Some CSRs have limited authority to handle routine claims, such as windshield damage claims. CSRs also answer telephone inquiries and perform routine processing and clerical tasks.

## Producers

Insurance producers are often involved in the claim handling process. Some insureds call their producer first when a loss occurs. Producers record these claims and may assist the insured in the claim process. Providing this service, beyond their primary role of locating insurance coverage, gives producers an opportunity to demonstrate their value to their customers.

Draft authority

The authority expressly given to an agent by an insurer allowing the agent to settle and pay certain types of claims up to a specified limit.

Most insurers who market insurance through independent agents give **draft authority** to selected producers to settle certain types of claims up to a specified amount, such as $2,500. Generally, producers can use draft authority only to handle claims that require no liability determination, such as claims for damage to an insured's own home or automobile. See the exhibit " Sample Claim Department Organizational Chart."

Authorized producers can issue drafts (checks) directly to insureds for covered claims. In this capacity, producers perform a role similar to that of a telephone claim representative, but usually only for small claims. If a producer does not have draft authority, the producer immediately reports the loss to the insurer, gives the insured the telephone number of the insurer's claim office, and explains how the insured can expect the claim to be handled.

## Sample Claim Department Organizational Chart

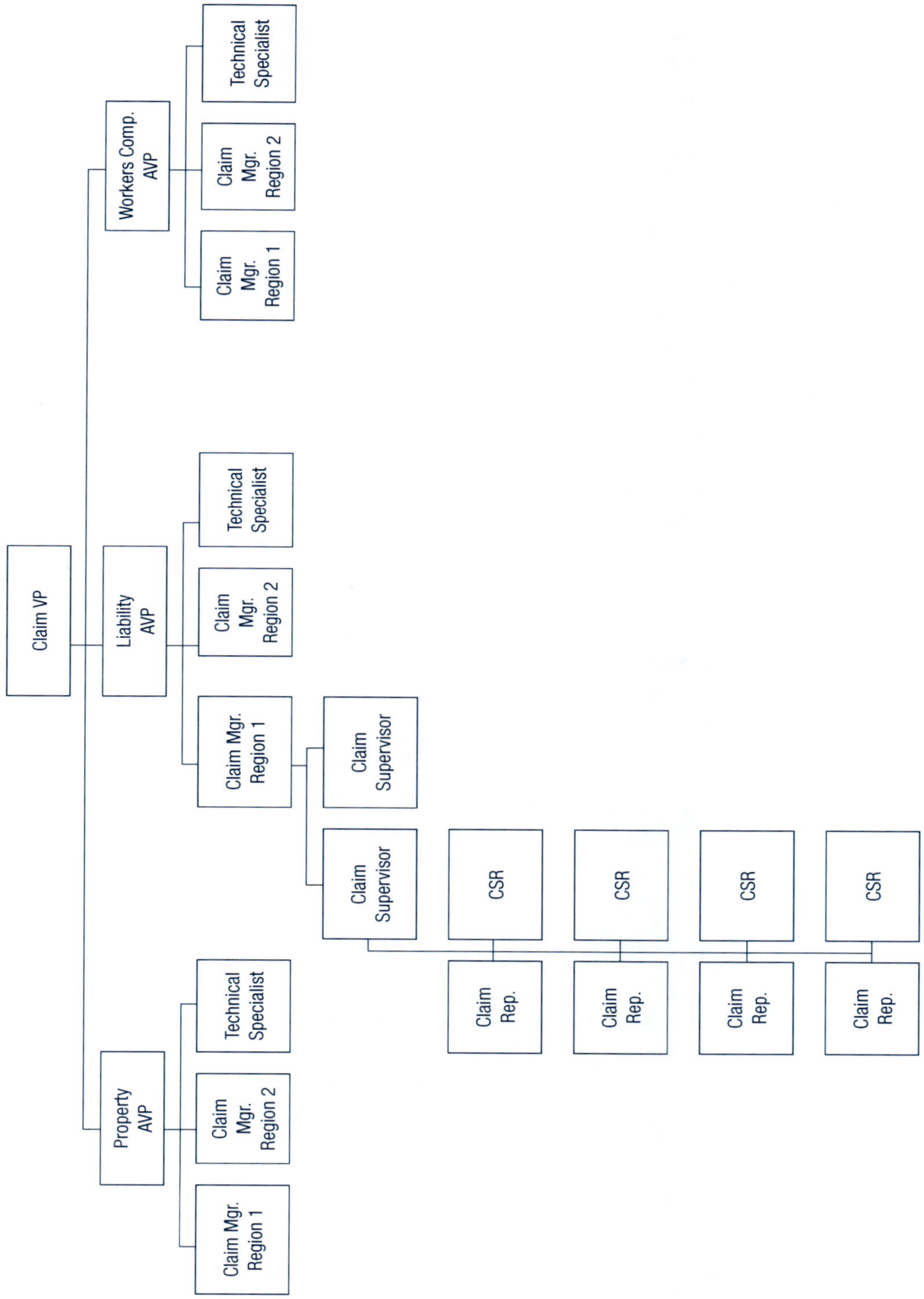


[DA00046]

# MEASURING CLAIM RESULTS

Insurers measure their claim results using internal standards to evaluate the claim function and individual claim representatives.

Managers in most insurance organizations develop goals for the organization, their departments, and individual staff members to ensure the organization's profit. An insurer's claim results, achieved by accomplishing the goals of the claim function, are a crucial factor in determining overall profitability. Both financial and nonfinancial tools are used to evaluate an insurer's claim results.

## Financial Tools

Managers periodically measure claim results using financial tools, including the loss ratio and analysis of reserving accuracy. The loss ratio is a measure of claim results and is calculated from incurred losses, including loss adjustment expenses (LAE), divided by earned premiums.

Over time, an insurer's loss ratio can increase, decrease, or remain stable. An increasing loss ratio can be a sign of an insurer's pending financial difficulties, a decreasing loss ratio can indicate that an insurer is becoming more profitable, and a stable loss ratio can indicate that an insurer's profitability is unchanged.

An increasing loss ratio can result from one or more factors. For example, the claim function could be operating inefficiently, underwriting could be selecting below-average loss exposures, or the pricing of the insurer's products may be inaccurate. See the exhibit "Balancing and Controlling Loss Adjustment Expenses."

### Balancing and Controlling Loss Adjustment Expenses

Good claim handling practices should not be sacrificed in order to reduce loss adjustment expenses. For example, paying demanded settlements without properly investigating claims would reduce the expenses of investigation; however, in the long term, it would result in greater settlement amounts, which would increase the loss ratio.

An insurer's claim handling guidelines provide claim handling policies and procedures that are designed to result in fair and effective claim settlement while minimizing expenses. Good-faith claim handling—considering the interests of the insured as much as the interests of the insurer—also helps control expenses by minimizing lawsuits and bad-faith claims against the insurer.

[DA07520]

The accuracy of loss reserves provides another financial tool to measure claim results. When claims are presented, claim staff set loss reserves and adjust these reserves throughout the claim handling process to ensure that the reserves continue to represent realistic estimates of the amount the insurer will pay. Reserves should provide managers with an accurate estimate of an insurer's liability for existing claims to ensure accuracy of an insurer's financial reporting. Most insurers provide reserve reports for claim managers to use in evaluating reserves.

To satisfy state insurance regulations, insurers must allocate funds on their **balance sheets** to cover reserve totals. Inadequate reserving may create an inaccurate impression of the insurer's financial worth as reflected on its financial statements.

**Balance sheet**
The financial statement that reports the assets, liabilities, and owners' equity of an organization as of a specific date.

## Nonfinancial Tools

Nonfinancial measures can also be used to evaluate claim results. Managers use nonfinancial measures to evaluate the effectiveness of the claim function and the performance of individual claim representatives. Nonfinancial measures commonly include best practices, other nonfinancial criteria, and customer feedback.

### Best Practices

In a claim department, best practices usually refer to a system of identified individual practices that produce superior performance. Best practices are usually documented and shared with all claim managers and claim representatives. Claim department best practices are generally based on a combination of legal requirements, such as **unfair claim practices laws**, and the insurer's own standards.

**Unfair claim practices law**
A state law that specifies illegal claim practices.

Best practices for claim departments address matters such as these:

- Timely claim acknowledgment
- Timely response to outside communications
- Timely loss reserving
- Timely payment or denial of claims
- Complete explanation of payments or denials
- File documentation standards

### Other Nonfinancial Tools

Other nonfinancial criteria for evaluating the claim function include these:

- Claim turnover—the average time it takes for open claims to be closed
- Number and percentage of litigated claims
- Ratio of successfully litigated claims to unsuccessfully litigated claims

- Average caseload per claim representative—the average number of claims each claim representative has open at any time
- Staff turnover—overall frequency of staff member changes resulting from retirements, other employment opportunities, and disciplinary actions

Nonfinancial criteria for evaluating individual claim representatives' performance include these:

- File turnover—the time it takes a claim representative to bring a claim to closure
- Ratio of litigated claims to nonlitigated claims
- Comparison of average settlement costs among claim representatives who handle similar claims

## Customer Feedback

Customer feedback and survey results often suggest ways in which the claim function can improve the customer experience and better serve insureds. Customer feedback can come from many sources, such as directly from an insured, a claimant, or a vendor; or indirectly from a state insurance department on behalf of an insured, a claimant, or a vendor. Claim management must investigate complaints submitted to a state insurance department and respond to them in a timely manner.

## Claim Audits

Claim audits can ensure compliance with best practices and also can be used to gather statistical information to evaluate other criteria, including the accuracy of reserves. Those who audit claims review a number of open and closed claim files, evaluating both qualitative and quantitative factors. Data derived from claim audits give insurance managers a snapshot of how well a claim department and individual claim representatives perform the claim function and, consequently, of the overall effectiveness of the claim function. Specific measures can reveal flaws in the claim handling process and identify areas where the department or individual claim representatives require further training or education.

# SUMMARY

The two primary goals of the claim function are keeping the insurer's promise and supporting the insurer's profit goal. Claim personnel help meet these goals by using the claim handling process to promptly, fairly, and equitably pay all legitimate first- and third-party claims and by managing operational and claim handling expenses. Policyholders' satisfaction that the insurer's contractual promises have been upheld promotes goodwill and supports an insurer's profit goals.

The activities in the claim handling process include acknowledging a claim and assigning it to a claim representative, identifying the policy, contacting the insured or the insured's representative, investigating and documenting the claim, determining cause of loss and loss amount, and concluding the claim. A basic understanding of these claim handling activities helps insurance professionals understand how an insurer complies with the contractual promise made in the insurance policy.

A variety of claim personnel collaborate to fulfill the contractual promise that insurers make to their insureds in insurance policies. Claim managers oversee various levels of the claim operation. Claim supervisors support the claim functions of the managers to whom they report. Claim representatives, including telephone claim representatives, field claim representatives, and technical specialists, investigate, evaluate, and settle claims. Customer service representatives perform routine processing and clerical tasks and may handle routine claims. Producers assist their insurance clients by recording claims and sometimes settling small claims.

An insurer's claim results help determine the insurer's success. Insurers can evaluate claim results through financial and nonfinancial tools. Financial tools include the insurer's loss ratio and reserving accuracy. Nonfinancial tools help an insurer evaluate both the claim function and the performance of individual claim representatives. Audits can be used to assess performance in both financial and nonfinancial areas.

Direct Your Learning

# 5

# Insurance Regulation

## Educational Objectives

After learning the content of this assignment, you should be able to:

- Explain why insurance operations are regulated.
- Explain how individual states in the United States regulate the licensing of insurers.
- Explain how individual states in the United States regulate insurance rates and policy forms.
- Explain how the individual states in the United States regulate market conduct and insurer solvency.

## Outline

# Insurance Regulation

5

## WHY INSURANCE OPERATIONS ARE REGULATED

When purchasing insurance, consumers may have many questions and concerns about whether the coverage they are purchasing will really protect them. Insurance regulation is meant to address many of these concerns.

Insurance consumers' concerns include whether the policy forms give them the coverage they expect and need, whether the price is appropriate, and whether the insurer will have the resources needed to pay losses that may occur months or even years after a policy has been purchased. To protect individuals, organizations, and entire communities from these kinds of problems, all of the states in the United States regulate insurance. Regulation varies considerably from state to state. However, most states focus their regulatory efforts on the same key areas of insurer operations: licensing, insurance rates, insurance policies, market conduct, and insurer solvency.

Insurers are regulated primarily for three reasons:

- To protect consumers
- To maintain insurer solvency
- To prevent destructive competition

### Protect Consumers

Insurance is regulated to protect consumers. Many insurance policies are complex legal documents that may be difficult for some consumers to analyze and understand. Regulators help protect consumers by reviewing insurance policy forms to determine whether they benefit consumers. Regulators can set coverage standards, specify policy language for certain insurance coverages, and disapprove unacceptable policies.

Insurance regulators also protect consumers against fraud and unethical market behavior by insurers and producers, such as selling unnecessary insurance, misrepresenting coverage to make a sale, or refusing to pay legitimate claims.

Regulators try to ensure that insurance is readily available, especially the insurance that is viewed as a necessity. For example, all states try to make personal auto insurance available by restricting the rights of insurers to cancel or refuse to renew personal auto insurance policies.

## Maintain Insurer Solvency

Solvency

The ability of an insurer to meet its financial obligations as they become due, even those resulting from insured losses that may be claimed several years in the future.

Insurance is regulated to maintain insurer **solvency**. Insurance regulators try to maintain and enhance the financial condition of private insurers for several reasons:

- Premiums are paid in advance, and the period of protection extends into the future. If an insurer becomes insolvent, future claims might not be paid even though the premium has been paid. Consumers may find it difficult to evaluate insurers' financial ability to keep their promises.
- Regulation is needed to protect the public interest. Large numbers of individuals are adversely affected when insurers become insolvent. For example, an unusually large catastrophe that affects a large area can make an insurer's financial ability to pay claims uncertain, such as when Hurricane Andrew struck Florida in 1992 and caused seven insurer insolvencies.
- Insurers hold substantial funds for the ultimate benefit of policyholders. Government regulation is necessary to safeguard such funds.

Despite regulatory reviews, insurers have become insolvent. However, sound regulation minimizes the number of insolvencies.

## Prevent Destructive Competition

Insurance is regulated to prevent destructive competition. Therefore, regulators are responsible for determining whether insurance rates are adequate.

At times, some insurers price their policies too low in an effort to attract customers away from higher-priced competitors. This practice drives down price levels in the whole insurance market. Therefore, when insurance rate levels become inadequate, some insurers may not collect enough money to pay all of their insureds' claims and may become insolvent. Other insurers might lose so much profit that they withdraw from the market or stop writing new business. An insurance shortage can then develop, and individuals and organizations might be unable to obtain the coverage they need.

For example, following periods of intense competition among insurers, pharmaceutical companies have found it difficult to obtain commercial liability insurance to cover the risk of product defects in the drugs they manufacture.

# INSURER LICENSING

Most insurance companies must be licensed by the state insurance department before they are authorized to write insurance policies in that state.

In the United States, insurers are licensed as domestic insurers in the states where they are domiciled. When insurers wish to operate in additional states, they become licensed as foreign insurers. Insurers domiciled outside the U.S.

are licensed as alien insurers. Surplus lines insurers typically operate through a specially licensed producer.

In addition to requiring that insurance companies (most commonly stock, mutual, or reciprocal exchange insurers) be licensed, states also generally require that certain individual insurance professionals, such as producers and claim representatives, be licensed.

## Insurer's Licensing Status

An insurer's licensing status in a given state may assume any one of several forms: that of a **domestic insurer**, a **foreign insurer**, or an **alien insurer**. Licensing standards vary among these several forms. For example, a domestic insurer's license generally has no expiration date, whereas licenses of a foreign insurer and an alien insurer generally must be renewed annually.

**Alien insurer**

An insurer domiciled in a country other than the United States.

**Foreign insurer**

An insurer licensed to operate in a state but incorporated in another state.

**Domestic insurer**

An insurer doing business in the jurisdiction in which it is incorporated.

## Becoming Licensed as a Domestic Insurer

Domestic insurers usually must meet the conditions imposed on corporations engaged in noninsurance activities as well as some additional conditions imposed on insurers. An applicant for a domestic insurer license must apply for a corporate charter and provide specific information, including (but not limited to) these items:

- The insurer's form of ownership
- The names and addresses of the individual incorporators
- The name of the proposed corporation and the territories and types of insurance it plans to market
- The insurer's total financing, including authorized capital stock (the total number of shares, if any, that a corporation can sell to raise money), and its policyholders' surplus

### Forms of Ownership

Insurers can be classified by legal form of ownership. The three most common forms of insurer ownership in the U.S. are stock insurance companies, mutual insurance companies, and reciprocal insurance exchanges.

Insurers formed for the purpose of making a profit for their owners are typically organized as **stock insurers**. Stockholders supply the capital needed to form the insurance company or the additional capital the insurer needs to expand its operations. Stockholders expect to receive a return on their investment in the form of stock dividends, increased stock value, or both. Stockholders have the right to elect the board of directors. The board of directors creates and oversees corporate goals and objectives and appoints a chief executive officer (CEO) to carry out the insurer's operations.

**Stock insurer**

An insurer that is owned by its stockholders and formed as a corporation for the purpose of earning a profit for the stockholders.

**Mutual insurer**

An insurer that is owned by its policyholders and formed as a corporation for the purpose of providing insurance to them.

A **mutual insurer** is a corporation owned by its policyholders. Because a traditional mutual insurer issues no common stock, it has no stockholders. Its policyholders have voting rights similar to those of a stock company's stockholders, and, like stockholders, they elect the insurer's board of directors. Although initially formed to provide insurance for their owners, mutual insurers today generally seek to earn profits in their ongoing operations, just as stock companies do. A mutual insurer needs profits to ensure the future financial health of the organization. Mutual companies include some large national insurers and many regional insurers.

A reciprocal insurance exchange, also referred to as a reciprocal, is organized as an unincorporated association of members, called subscribers, that agree to insure one another and share profits and losses. The term "reciprocal" comes from the reciprocity of responsibility of all subscribers to each other. Each member of the reciprocal is both an insured and an insurer. Because the subscribers are not experts in running an insurance operation, they contract with an individual or organization to operate the reciprocal. This manager, called an attorney-in-fact, is typically a corporation with a board of directors that manages the reciprocal. See the exhibit "Forms of Insurer Ownership."

### Forms of Insurer Ownership

| Type of Insurer | Form of Ownership | Managed by |
|---|---|---|
| Stock insurer | Corporation owned by its stockholders | Board of directors, elected by the stockholders |
| Mutual insurer | Corporation owned by its policyholders | Board of directors, elected by the policyholders |
| Reciprocal insurance exchange | Unincorporated association of subscribers | Attorney-in-fact chosen by the subscribers |

[DA07488]

## Capital and Surplus

Information about capital stock and surplus is important to licensing regulators because it indicates the insurer's financial soundness. A domestic insurer that is also a stock insurer must meet certain minimum capital and surplus requirements, which vary widely by state and by amounts and types of insurance written. A domestic insurer that is also a mutual insurer has no capital derived from the sale of stock. Therefore, the minimum financial requirement applies only to surplus. Most states require mutual insurers to have an initial surplus equal to the minimum capital and surplus requirement for stock insurers writing the same type of insurance.

## Becoming Licensed as a Foreign or an Alien Insurer

In the U.S., an insurer is typically licensed as a domestic insurer in one state and as a foreign insurer in all other states where it wishes to operate. Less commonly, an insurer is domiciled outside the U.S. and is licensed as an alien insurer in the U.S. states where it wishes to operate.

To be licensed in an additional state (that is, as a foreign insurer), an insurer first must show the regulator in the additional state that it has satisfied the requirements imposed by its home state (its state of domicile, or the state where it is a domestic insurer). A foreign insurer also must generally satisfy the minimum capital, surplus, and other requirements imposed on domestic insurers within the state in which it is seeking to be licensed.

Alien insurers must satisfy the requirements imposed on domestic insurers by the state in which they want to be licensed. Additionally, they must usually establish a branch office in any state and have funds on deposit in the U.S. equal to the minimum capital and surplus required. The funds on deposit are available, if necessary, to pay claims asserted against the alien insurer through the U.S. legal system. See the exhibit "Licensing Status of a Hypothetical Insurer."

## Admitted Insurers and Nonadmitted Insurers

Insurers that are licensed to do business in a state, whether as domestic, foreign, or alien insurers, are collectively referred to as **admitted insurers**. Under special circumstances, insurers that are not licensed in the particular state, referred to as **nonadmitted insurers**, may be permitted to sell insurance within that state. A nonadmitted insurer may be an admitted insurer in other states, or it may even be an alien insurer.

Nonadmitted insurers are frequently referred to as surplus lines insurers. Surplus lines insurers are usually permitted to sell only insurance that is not readily available from admitted insurers because of specialty, risk, or several other factors. Under **surplus lines laws**, a nonadmitted insurer is permitted to transact business only through a specially licensed surplus lines producer. The nonadmitted insurer must still meet some of the regulatory requirements of a licensed insurer, but these do not typically include restrictions on rates and policy forms.

**Admitted insurer**
An insurer to which a state insurance department has granted a license to do business within that state.

**Nonadmitted insurer**
An insurer not authorized by the state insurance department to do business within that state.

**Surplus lines laws**
State laws that permit producers with a surplus lines license to write business for an acceptable "nonadmitted insurer when protection from admitted insurers is not available."

## Producers and Claim Representatives

In addition to licensing insurers, all states require licensing of certain insurer representatives or employees. Agents, brokers, and claim representatives are often required to pass an examination on insurance laws and practices to earn a license. These examinations, along with continuing education requirements, are an attempt to ensure that these insurance professionals have a minimum level of insurance knowledge and meet ethical standards.

## Licensing Status of a Hypothetical Insurer

Insurer A, a regional insurer domiciled in Ohio, is licensed as a domestic insurer in Ohio and is licensed as a foreign insurer in its other states of operation.

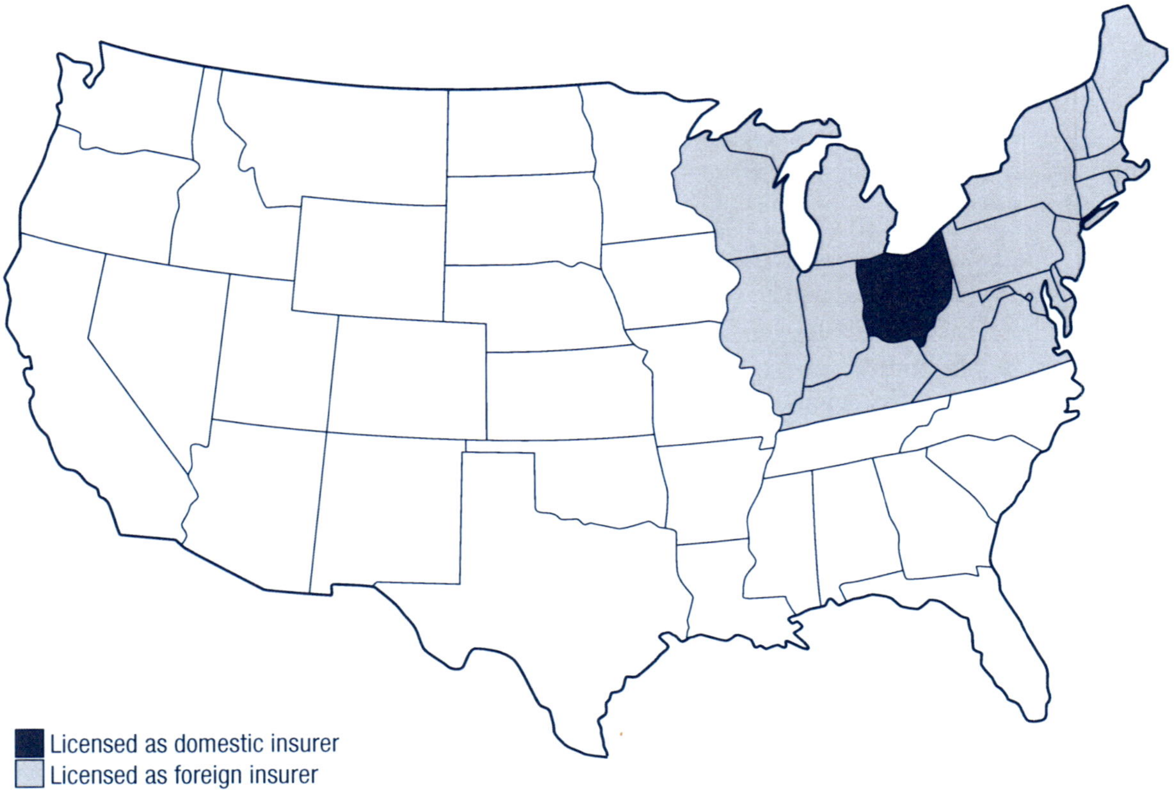


[DA07504]

# INSURANCE RATE AND FORM REGULATION

Individual states in the United States regulate insurance rates to strike a balance between reasonable profits for insurers and reasonable prices for consumers. Additionally, states regulate insurance policy forms to ensure that they are readable, understandable, and fair.

A solvent, profitable insurance market that provides insurance products at affordable rates is important to the citizens of every state. From coverage on their homes and autos to workers compensation, individuals need insurance. Organizations of all types and sizes cannot operate without insurance. Because insurance is important and often required for individuals and businesses, states enact laws to ensure that rates are sufficient for insurers and reasonable for consumers.

In addition to being able to afford to purchase insurance, consumers also need to be able to understand the insurance products they purchase. Therefore, states typically regulate insurance policy forms to enable consumers to read and understand them. Methods of regulation include requiring certain language or provisions, or mandating that a particular policy form be used. Most states review policy provisions to ensure that they are fair and reasonable.

There are, however, certain types of insurance, such as coverage for complex commercial organizations or unique risks, exempted from regulation.

## Insurance Rate Regulation

Setting insurance rates is the regulatory area that may receive the most public attention. It is important to insurers that rates allow them to collect sufficient premiums to pay for the insured losses that occur, to cover the insurer's costs of operating, and to allow a reasonable profit.

When deciding to approve or disapprove an insurer's request for a rate, a state insurance commissioner usually considers three major criteria:

- Adequate—Rates should be sufficient to pay all claims and the expenses related to those claims, helping to maintain insurer solvency.
- Not excessive—Insurers are entitled to a fair return but not to excessive or unreasonable profit.
- Not unfairly discriminatory—Insurers are permitted to adjust premium rates based on the risk profile of different groups of insureds, but these rates must be fair and consistent. Insureds with similar loss exposures should be charged similar rates.

Different states meet these criteria by different types of rating laws that vary in the type and extent of control the state asserts over insurers' rates:

- **Mandatory rate law**—Rate law that imposes the strictest control of an insurer's rates.
- **Prior-approval law**—Insurers cannot charge a rate until it is approved by state regulators.
- **File-and-use law**—Insurers must file proposed rates, but can use the rates while state approval is pending.
- **Use-and-file law**—Variation of the file-and-use law that provides more flexibility for insurers in setting rates.
- **Flex rating law**—Increases the amount of flexibility for insurers in their rate determinations.
- **Open competition**—Market prices driven by the economic laws of supply and demand, rather than regulatory decisions, determine insurance rates. However, state insurance departments typically have the authority to monitor competition and disapprove rates if deemed necessary. The major criteria that rates must be adequate, not excessive, and not unfairly discriminatory continue to apply.

**Mandatory rate law**
State law under which insurance rates are set by a state agency or rating bureau and all licensed insurers are required to use those rates.

**Prior-approval law**
An insurance rating law in which the rates and supporting rules must be filed with and approved by the state insurance department before they can be used.

**File-and-use law**
An insurance rating law in which the insurer must file rates and supporting rules with the state insurance department prior to their use, but the rates can then be used immediately without specific approval.

**Use-and-file law**
An insurance rating law in which the rates must be filed with the state insurance department within a specified period after they are put into use.

**Flex rating law**
An insurance rating law under which prior approval is required only if the new rates exceed a certain percentage above (and sometimes below) the rates previously filed.

**Open competition**
An insurance rating law that allows insurers to develop and use rates without having to file with or get approval from the state insurance department.

## Insurance Policy Form Regulation

Another area of insurance regulation involves insurance policy forms. Because many insurance policies are difficult to interpret and are often sold on a take-it-or-leave-it basis, many states require insurers to file their policy forms with the state insurance department.

Regulations regarding insurance policy forms are intended to meet two major objectives. The first objective is that insurance policies be clear and readable to insurance consumers. The second major objective is to detect and address any policy provisions that are unfair or unreasonable.

Some state legislatures enact laws that control the structure and content of insurance policies. Such laws may require the use of a specific form or provision in all policies of a certain type that are sold in the state. For example, many states require the use of a standard workers compensation policy that provides coverage for on-the-job injuries. Some state laws require insurance policies to meet a readability test. The requirements for readability may include the use of common, easily understood language and specific policy style, form, and print size.

## Exemptions From Rate and Form Regulation

State insurance regulations do not apply to all insurers and insurance. Some insurers and some types of insurance policies are exempt from regulation regarding premium rates and policy forms.

Surplus lines insurers are generally exempt from insurance regulations pertaining to policy forms and rates. These insurers are willing to provide coverage for risks that admitted insurers are unable or unwilling to offer. Because these insurers increase the availability of insurance, they have the freedom to use policy provisions and rates that are appropriate for a particular risk.

There are various types of coverage related to unique or difficult-to-place risks that are also exempt from regulation in some states. Examples of these coverages include inland marine, ocean marine, and aviation. Inland marine originated and evolved in order to cover risks that were considered uninsurable under standard commercial policies, such as coverage for works of art and other valuable property.

Many states have deregulated some commercial insurance coverages for large, sophisticated purchasers. There is significant variation in the definition of the size of business to qualify for exemption from rate and form regulation. One state, for example, may require an aggregate annual premium of $500,000, while another state could require $25,000. Many states do not exempt certain types of commercial coverage, such as workers compensation or commercial property, from regulation.

# MARKET CONDUCT AND SOLVENCY REGULATION

States regulate how insurers conduct themselves in the marketplace and monitor their financial strength for the protection of the public and insurance consumers.

States have consumer protection laws that apply directly to insurers conducting business within their borders. Solvency regulations that establish insurer financial requirements and monitoring systems seek to protect the public from loss of insurance coverage in the event of an insurer's financial failure.

## Market Conduct

**Market conduct regulation** focuses on insurers' treatment of applicants for insurance, insureds, and others who present claims for coverage. Most states have statutes that address market conduct, often called **unfair trade practices laws**. These laws usually involve three areas of insurance company operations: sales, underwriting, and claim handling.

Market conduct regulation

Regulation of the practices of insurers in regard to four areas of operation: sales practices, underwriting practices, claim practices, and bad-faith actions.

Unfair trade practices law

State law that specifies certain prohibited business practices.

### Sales and Underwriting

State regulators can suspend or revoke the licenses of sales agents or brokers who engage in unfair trade practices, such as embezzling premiums. Similarly, an insurer that is guilty of unfair underwriting practices could be fined, or its operating license in a state could be suspended or revoked. Under the unfair trade practices acts, examples of improper underwriting include unfair discrimination and canceling or not renewing policies, contrary to state regulations.

### Claims

Most states also have statutes that prohibit unfair claim practices and assess fines against claim representatives and insurers that engage in practices such as intentionally making unfairly low settlement offers, failing to provide reasonable explanations for denying a claim, misrepresenting important policy provisions, or failing to approve or deny coverage within a reasonable time period.

Regulatory examinations of insurers identify some of these abuses, but others are exposed only when an insured or a claimant lodges a complaint. Every state insurance department has a consumer complaints division to enforce its consumer protection objectives and to help insureds deal with problems they have encountered with insurers and their representatives. State insurance departments investigate consumer complaints and may hold formal hearings as part of the investigation process.

## Insurer Solvency

Another area of insurance regulation is insurer solvency. A noninsurance company is considered solvent if it has resources to pay its bills and meet similar financial obligations. Because an insurer has promised to pay many unknown losses in the future, states require it to have financial reserves well in excess of its ordinary expenses in order to be considered solvent. See the exhibit "Causes of Insurer Insolvencies."

### Causes of Insurer Insolvencies

Mismanagement in some form is at the root of most insurer insolvencies. Primary causes of insurer insolvencies in recent years have been deficient loss reserves, inadequate pricing, and rapid growth. Less frequent causes include investment problems, alleged fraud, and catastrophe losses.

A.M. Best Company, 2010 Special Report: U.S. Surplus Lines—Market Review (Oldwick, N.J.: A.M. Best Company, September 2010), p. 29. [DA07446]

Solvency surveillance

The process, conducted by state insurance regulators, of verifying the solvency of insurers and determining whether their financial condition enables them to meet their financial obligations and to remain in business.

Solvency for an insurer is its ability to meet its financial obligations as they become due, even those resulting from insured losses that might be claimed several years in the future. To verify insurer solvency, insurance regulators conduct **solvency surveillance**.

Regulators use four methods to verify the solvency of insurers:

- Establish financial requirements by which to measure solvency
- Conduct on-site field examinations to ensure regulatory compliance
- Review annual financial statements
- Administer the Insurance Regulatory Information System (IRIS)

### Establish Financial Requirements

Regulators establish financial requirements against which all similarly licensed insurers are measured. To obtain and keep a license as an admitted insurer, each insurer must meet certain minimum financial requirements, such as capital and surplus requirements. Specific financial requirements vary widely by state.

### Conduct Field Examinations

State laws usually require that insurers undergo on-site field examinations at least once every three to five years. This examination usually occurs under the direction of the insurance department of the state where the insurer's home office is located.

A team of state examiners, working at the insurance company home office, reviews a wide range of activities, including claim, underwriting, marketing, and accounting procedures. Of particular interest to the examiners is the insurer's financial condition. The examining team carefully analyzes the insurer's financial records to ensure that the company is meeting all state financial reporting requirements.

## Review Annual Statements

Insurers are required to submit annual financial statements to state insurance departments in a prescribed format. The **National Association of Insurance Commissioners (NAIC)** has prescribed a format called the **NAIC Annual Statement**, which requires detailed information on premiums, expenses, investments, losses, **reserves**, and other financial information. Regulators analyze these statements to assess insurers' financial strength.

## Administer IRIS

Regulators administer the **Insurance Regulatory Information System (IRIS)**, which helps them identify insurers with potential financial problems. Designed by the NAIC, IRIS uses data from an insurer's financial statements to develop financial ratios that assess the insurer's overall financial condition. If the insurer has ratios that are outside predetermined norms, IRIS identifies the company for regulatory attention. IRIS is meant to be an early warning system that might enable regulators to rehabilitate an insurer or, if rehabilitation is not practical, to minimize the losses from liquidation.

If regulators determine that an insurer is insolvent, the state insurance department places it in receivership. If the insurer cannot be rehabilitated, it is liquidated according to the state's insurance code. At that point, the state's **guaranty fund** may be available to reduce the effects of the insurer insolvency. A guaranty fund cannot prevent insurer insolvency, but it does provide funds to pay unpaid claims of insolvent insurers licensed in a particular state.

Under a special provision in state insurer licensing laws, state regulators are empowered to partially or completely take over the operation of an insurer that has been determined to be in danger of failing to meet its financial obligations. In extreme cases, a state may even dissolve an insurer and assign administration of the existing policies to another insurer.

# SUMMARY

Insurers are regulated primarily for these three reasons:

- To protect consumers
- To maintain insurer solvency
- To prevent destructive competition

Insurers must meet various requirements to be licensed as domestic insurers in the states where they are domiciled. Additionally, insurers must also

**National Association of Insurance Commissioners (NAIC)**

An association of insurance commissioners from the fifty U.S. states, the District of Columbia, and the five U.S. territories and possessions, whose purpose is to coordinate insurance regulation activities among the various state insurance departments.

**NAIC Annual Statement**

The primary financial statement prepared by insurers and required by every state insurance department.

**Reserve**

The amount the insurer estimates and sets aside to pay on an existing claim that has not been settled.

**Insurance Regulatory Information System (IRIS)**

An information and early-warning system established and operated by the NAIC to monitor the financial soundness of insurers.

**Guaranty fund**

A state-established fund that provides a system for the payment of some of the unpaid claims of insolvent insurers licensed in that state, generally funded by assessments collected from all insurers licensed in the state.

be licensed as foreign insurers in other states where they wish to operate. Nonadmitted insurers may transact certain types of business through licensed surplus lines producers. In addition to requiring that insurers be licensed, states also require that certain insurance professionals, including producers and claim representatives, become licensed.

States regulate insurance rates to ensure that they are adequate, not excessive, and not unfairly discriminatory. States also regulate insurance policy forms to meet standards of clarity, fairness, and readability. However, there are certain types of insurance, such as large commercial policies or unique coverages, that are exempt from state regulation.

States regulate insurers' market conduct, focusing on insurers' treatment of applicants for insurance, insureds, and others who present claims for coverage. Market conduct regulation, which includes unfair trade practices laws and unfair claim practices laws, usually applies to three areas of insurance company operations: sales, underwriting, and claim handling.

State solvency laws seek to ensure the financial strength of insurers so that they can meet their obligations to insureds and claimants. Solvency regulators establish insurer financial requirements, conduct field examinations, review annual financial statements, and administer the Insurance Regulatory Information System, which identifies insurers in danger of becoming insolvent.

# Direct Your Learning

# 6

## Insurance Policies

### Educational Objectives

After learning the content of this assignment, you should be able to:

- Explain how insurance policies can be structured using each of these alternatives:
  - Preprinted and manuscript forms
  - Self-contained and modular policies
  - Endorsements and other related documents
- Given a specific policy provision, classify it into one of the following categories:
  - Declarations
  - Definitions
  - Insuring agreements
  - Conditions
  - Exclusions
  - Miscellaneous provisions
- Explain how to read an insurance policy to determine whether a claim is covered and, if so, for what amount.

### Outline

# Insurance Policies

# 6

## INSURANCE POLICY STRUCTURE

An insurance policy is a carefully written contract that describes the agreement between the insured individual or organization and the insurer. Insurers use different types of policy structure to meet insureds' particular needs.

Insurance policy structure can vary, depending on customer coverage needs. Most policies are issued using **preprinted forms**, but **manuscript forms** may be used when an insured has coverage needs that preprinted forms do not adequately address. Moreover, all policies can be classified as being either **self-contained policies** or **modular policies**. Another important aspect of policy structure is the incorporation of endorsements or other documents into the policy.

**Manuscript form**
An insurance form that is drafted according to terms negotiated between a specific insured (or group of insureds) and an insurer.

**Preprinted form**
An insurance form that meets the needs of many policyholders and is therefore printed in bulk for future use.

**Self-contained policy**
A single document that contains all the agreements between the insured and the insurer and that forms a complete insurance policy.

**Modular policy**
An insurance policy that consists of several different documents, none of which by itself forms a complete policy.

### Preprinted and Manuscript Forms

Depending on whether the insurer can use a form already created or must create a new form for a customer, the policy can be either a preprinted form or a manuscript form.

Most insurers use standard preprinted policy forms, because it is not necessary to negotiate new contractual terms for each policy purchased. Insurance advisory organizations, such as Insurance Services Office, Inc. (ISO) and the American Association of Insurance Services (AAIS), develop industry-wide standardized forms for different types of property-casualty insurance, and many insurers use these standard forms. Alternatively, an insurer may develop its own nonstandard, preprinted forms. For example, a person buying auto insurance may find that three small insurers are using the same ISO standard policy form, but that one large insurer is using its own nonstandard, preprinted policy form for auto coverage.

When an insurer's preprinted forms do not provide the terms of coverage needed by a particular insured or a small group of insureds, the insurer (or in some cases the insured's broker) may draft a manuscript form to meet the customers' needs. For example, an insurer might develop a manuscript form to cover the unique liability exposures of a highly specialized profession. Because of the limited number of professionals requiring this coverage, insurers typically would not have preprinted forms available for that class of insureds.

## Self-Contained and Modular Policies

Depending on the type and variety of coverages a customer seeks, a policy can be a single document (self-contained), or it may require a combination of documents to include all the agreements between the insured and the insurer (modular).

If the customer seeks coverage that is common to a large number of insureds, the insurer may choose to offer a self-contained policy. A personal auto policy is an example of a self-contained policy. Because most drivers have very similar auto insurance needs, a self-contained personal auto policy serves the needs of most insureds.

Conversely, if the customer seeks a variety of coverages that may not be common to a large number of insureds, the insurer may choose to offer a modular policy to tailor a policy to an insured's specific needs.

The ISO commercial package policy (CPP) is an example of a modular policy because it combines different **coverage parts** to meet the insured's particular needs. Commercial insureds' needs can vary, depending on the type of business insured. For example, some businesses may need commercial auto coverage, and others may not. See the exhibit "Components of the ISO Commercial Package Policy."

Coverage part

A component of a CPP or a monoline policy that contains the policy provisions relating to a particular line of business, such as commercial property or commercial general liability; consists of the coverage part's declarations page, one or more coverage forms, applicable endorsements, and in some cases a general provisions form.

Each ISO-type CPP begins with two component documents: a set of common policy conditions and common declarations. Adding the necessary forms to make up the coverage parts that meet the insured's needs completes the policy. In most cases, a separate **declarations page** is included for each coverage part contained in the CPP.

Declarations page (declarations, or dec.)

An insurance policy information page or pages providing specific details about the insured and the subject of the insurance.

## Endorsements and Other Related Documents

Documents other than insurance forms can become part of a policy either by being physically attached to, or by being referenced within, the policy. Documents that can become part of a policy are the completed application, endorsements, the insurer's bylaws, and relevant statutory terms or provisions. See the exhibit "Related Insurance Policy Documents."

An insurance application, the documented request for coverage, contains information about the insured and the loss exposures presented to the insurer. The insurer usually keeps the completed application in order to preserve the insured's representations. In some cases, misleading or false representations in an application can be grounds for denying a claim. Some state statutes require that any written application become part of the policy for some types of insurance.

An **endorsement** adds to or modifies an insurance policy. An endorsement may be a few words handwritten into a policy, or it may be a separate document of one or more pages—preprinted, computer-printed, typewritten, or handwritten—that is attached to the policy.

Endorsement

A document that amends an insurance policy.

## Components of the ISO Commercial Package Policy

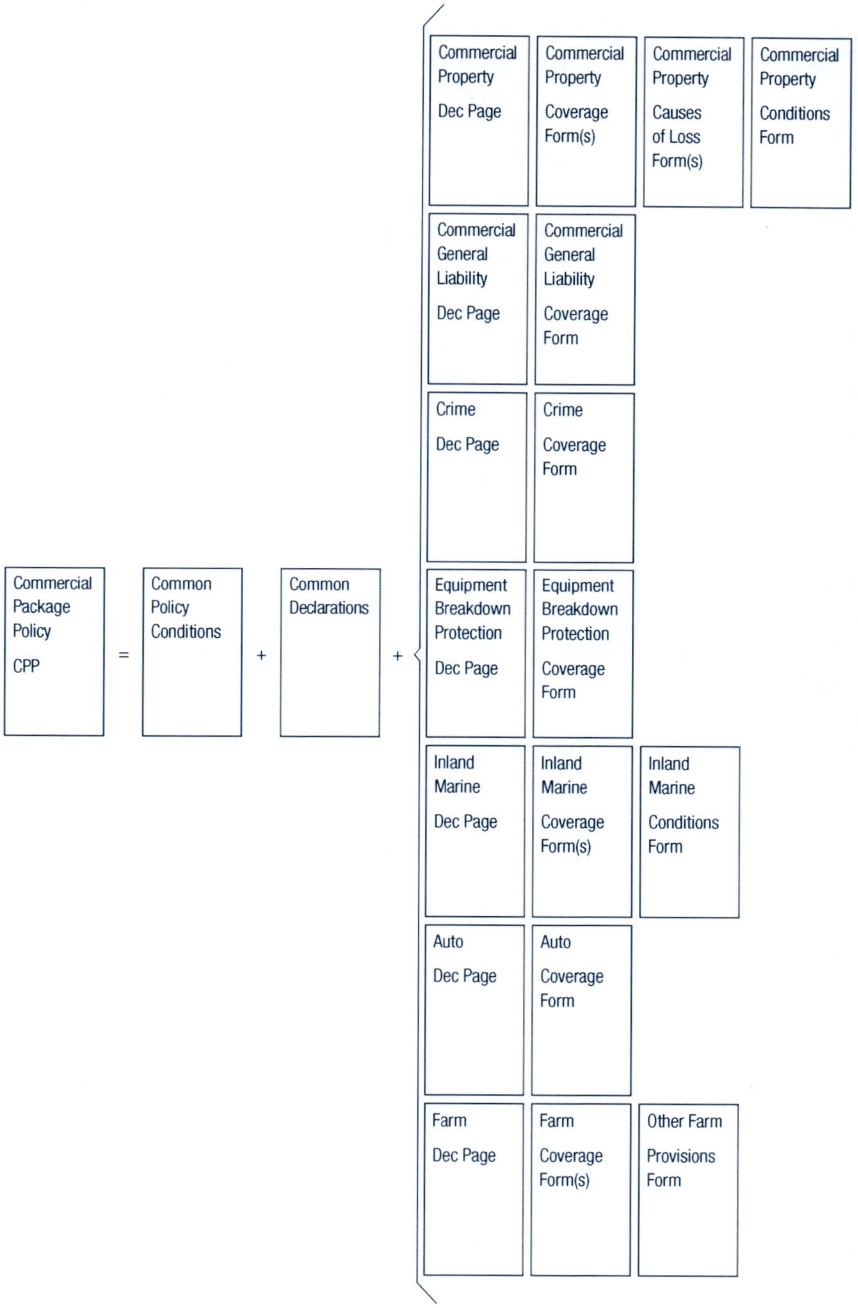


[DA00427]

## Related Insurance Policy Documents

| Related document | Description | Example |
|---|---|---|
| Application | Documented request for coverage, containing information about insured and loss exposures | Personal auto policy application containing relevant insured information pertinent to driving and vehicle/s |
| Endorsements | Documents modifying basic policy form | Homeowners policy endorsement for home business coverage |
| Insurer's bylaws | Insurer's corporate bylaws | Attachment to policy issued by mutual insurer giving insureds corporate rights |
| Relevant statutory terms | Incorporation of statute by reference in policy | Workers compensation or no-fault auto insurance statutes |

[DA00429]

An endorsement's provisions may conflict with the provisions of the policy to which the endorsement is attached. For example, a preprinted policy form may contain an exclusion, and an endorsement attached to the policy may delete the exclusion. If the policy and the endorsement contain conflicting terms, the endorsement takes precedence. Agreements between an insurer and insured, particularly handwritten alterations, tend to reflect true intent more accurately than do other, preprinted policy terms.

Some insurance contracts incorporate the insurer's bylaws or pertinent statutory provisions. For example, mutual and reciprocal insurance policyholders typically have rights and duties associated with managing the insurer's operations; the policy specifies these rights and duties by incorporating corporate documents.

Policies providing workers compensation insurance or auto no-fault insurance are among those that provide benefits required by state statutes. The insurance policy usually does not contain the relevant statutes but incorporates them by reference. For example, a standard workers compensation policy issued by the National Council on Compensation Insurance (NCCI) contains the following statement instead of detailing the types and amounts of benefits payable:

We will pay promptly when due the benefits required of you by the workers compensation law.

### *Apply Your Knowledge*

BNY Company has unique property and liability loss exposures that are not adequately insured under standard property-casualty insurance policies. What type of property-casualty policy would be the best solution for BNY?

a. Self-contained policy
b. Modular policy
c. Manuscript policy
d. Preprinted policy

*Feedback:* c. Because BNY Company has unique loss exposures, a manuscript policy would enable the insurer to draft a one-of-a-kind policy to address BNY's insurance needs.

# POLICY PROVISIONS

Policy provisions are insurance policy statements communicating the terms of the insurer's and insured's coverage agreements. They describe and clarify the insurance policy's coverage, the types of losses the policy does not cover, and the parties' contractual responsibilities.

Each **policy provision** typically fits within one of six categories, depending on the provision's purpose. Some policy provisions appear in policy sections matching the provision's category, such as a definition located in the policy's definitions section. Other policy provisions may be interspersed throughout the policy.

Policy provisions
Any phrase or clause in an insurance policy that describes the policy's coverages, exclusions, limits, conditions, or other features.

Common policy provisions fall within these six categories:

- Declarations
- Definitions
- Insuring agreements
- Conditions
- Exclusions
- Miscellaneous provisions

## Declarations

An insurance policy first must identify the parties to the contract. Information specific to the policy, such as the insurer's and insured's names and locations and the subject of insurance, usually appear on the policy's first page, usually called the declarations page, or simply the declarations. See the exhibit "Categories of Property-Casualty Insurance Policy Provisions."

## Categories of Property-Casualty Insurance Policy Provisions

| Category | Description | Effect on Coverage |
|---|---|---|
| Declarations | Unique information on the insured; list of forms included in policy | Outline who or what is covered, and where and when coverage applies |
| Definitions | Words with special meanings in policy | May limit or expand coverage based on definitions of terms |
| Insuring Agreements | Statements containing insurer's promise to make payment | State circumstances under which the insurer agrees to pay |
| Conditions | Qualifications on promise to make payment | Outline steps insured needs to take to enforce policy |
| Exclusions | Provisions stating what the insurer will not cover | Eliminates coverage for excluded persons, places, things, or actions |
| Miscellaneous Provisions | Wide variety of provisions that may alter policy | Deal with the relationship between the insured and the insurer or establish procedures for implementing the policy |

[DA00443]

The purpose of the declarations is to personalize a policy and tailor it to fit a particular policyholder's needs. The declarations contain (declare) information about the insured from the insurance application. They also summarize the coverage provided under the policy, along with other information unique to the policy. See the exhibit "Homeowners Policy Declarations."

## Homeowners Policy Declarations

# Homeowners Policy Declarations

**POLICYHOLDER: (Named Insured)** David M. and Joan G. Smith
216 Brookside Drive
Anytown, USA 40000

**POLICY NUMBER:** 296 H 578661

**POLICY PERIOD:** **Inception:** March 30, 20XX
**Expiration:** March 30, 20XX

**Policy period begins 12:01 A.M. standard time at the residence premises.**

**FIRST MORTGAGEE AND MAILING ADDRESS:**

Federal National Mortgage Assn.
C/O Mortgagee, Inc.
P.O. Box 5000
Businesstown, USA 55000

**We will provide the insurance described in this policy in return for the premium and compliance with all applicable policy provisions.**

| SECTION I COVERAGES | LIMIT |
|---|---|
| A—Dwelling | $ 120,000 |
| B—Other Structures | $ 12,000 |
| C—Personal Property | $ 60,000 |
| D—Loss of Use | $ 36,000 |

**SECTION I DEDUCTIBLE:** $ 250
**(In case of loss under Section I, we cover only that part of the loss over the deductible amount shown above.)**

| SECTION II COVERAGES | LIMIT | |
|---|---|---|
| E—Personal Liability | $ 300,000 | Each Occurrence |
| F—Medical Payments to Others | $ 1,000 | Each Person |

**CONSTRUCTION:** Masonry Veneer **NO. FAMILIES:** One **TYPE ROOF:** Approved

**YEAR BUILT:** 1990 **PROTECTION CLASS:** 7 **FIRE DISTRICT:** Cook Township

**NOT MORE THAN 1000 FEET FROM HYDRANT**

**NOT MORE THAN 5 MILES FROM FIRE DEPT.**

**FORMS AND ENDORSEMENTS IN POLICY:** HO 00 03, HO 04 61

**POLICY PREMIUM:** $ 350.00 **COUNTERSIGNATURE DATE:** **AGENT:** A.M. Abel

The declarations page typically contains these items:

- Policy number
- Policy inception and expiration dates
- Insurer's name
- Producer's name
- Named insured (policyholder's name)
- Named insured's mailing address
- Physical address and description of covered property or operations
- Numbers and edition dates of all attached forms and endorsements
- Dollar amounts of applicable policy limits
- Dollar amounts of applicable deductibles
- Names of persons or organizations whose additional interests the policy covers (such as mortgagees, loss payees, or additional insureds)
- Premium amount
- Any optional coverages the applicant has chosen

Scheduled coverage

Insurance for property specifically listed (scheduled) on a policy, with a limit of liability for each item.

Policy forms or endorsements also may contain information that qualifies as declarations, often in the form of **scheduled coverage**. For example, a homeowner might want increased limits of theft coverage for antique silverware stored in the home. A policy endorsement would list the details for such increased limits in a personal property schedule.

## Definitions

Most insurance policies contain a definitions section defining policy terms to help clarify real or perceived ambiguity. This section is usually located near the beginning or the end of a policy.

A policy's definitions section defines words and expressions having specific meaning within the policy. In some policies, defined words may appear in boldface or within quotation marks every time the policy uses them with the specified meaning.

## Insuring Agreements

Insuring agreement

A statement in an insurance policy that the insurer will, under described circumstances, make a loss payment or provide a service.

The purpose of an **insuring agreement**, which often follows the declarations and sometimes follows the definitions section, is to state in broad terms the insurer's promises to the insured. A policy providing more than one coverage can have more than one insuring agreement. For example, the Personal Auto Policy (PAP) contains provisions for liability, medical payments, uninsured motorists, and physical damage coverages, and each coverage has its own insuring agreement.

An insuring agreement usually introduces a coverage section, but it also can introduce other policy sections, such as coverage extensions, additional coverages, and supplementary payments.

An insuring agreement introducing a coverage section broadly states what the insurer agrees to do under the policy, subject to clarification in other parts of the policy, such as the policy definitions. Insuring agreements usually contain one or more defined terms crucial to understanding the coverage.

## Conditions

A policy's **conditions** section clarifies the insurer's and insured's duties, rights, and options. Some policy conditions are included in a policy's conditions section; others may be found in the forms, endorsements, or other documents that together make up the entire insurance policy.

Condition

Any provision in an insurance policy that qualifies an otherwise enforceable promise of the insurer.

The insured must comply with conditions for a policy to cover a loss. The insurer is obligated to perform its promise only if the insured has fulfilled its contractual duties as specified in the policy conditions.

The insurer's obligations, as stated in the insuring agreement, may include these duties:

- To pay covered losses
- To defend the insured from lawsuits
- To provide other services to the insured

The insured's obligations, which stem from the policy conditions, include these:

- To pay premiums
- To report losses promptly
- To provide appropriate documentation for losses
- To cooperate with the insurer, as in legal proceedings, for example
- To refrain from jeopardizing an insurer's rights to recover from responsible third parties (subrogate)

If the insured fails to perform these duties, the insurer might be released from its policy obligations.

## Exclusions

**Exclusions** are policy provisions that state what the insurer will not cover. The primary function of exclusions is not only to limit coverage but also to clarify the coverages granted by the insurer.

Exclusion

A policy provision that eliminates coverage for specified exposures.

An exclusion can serve one or more of these purposes:

- Eliminate coverage for uninsurable loss exposures—Some loss exposures are not generally insurable. Exclusions allow insurers to eliminate coverage for causes of loss that are difficult to insure, such as war, earthquake, or flood.
- Assist in managing moral hazards—Exaggerated or intentionally caused losses for the purpose of collecting insurance proceeds may be the result

Moral hazard

A condition that increases the likelihood that a person will intentionally cause or exaggerate a loss.

Morale hazard (attitudinal hazard)

A condition of carelessness or indifference that increases the frequency or severity of loss.

of **moral hazards** such as poor financial condition or a history of dishonesty. Exclusions help insurers minimize loss exposures that are affected by moral hazards.

- Assist in managing morale hazards—Losses often arise from carelessness or indifference because an individual is insured, reflecting **morale, or attitudinal, hazards**. Exclusions help insurers minimize loss exposures that are affected by morale hazards.
- Reduce the likelihood of coverage duplications—Sometimes two types of insurance policies may cover the same loss. Exclusions ensure that policies work together to provide complementary, but not duplicate, coverages.
- Eliminate coverages that the typical insured does not need—Exclusions can allow insurers to exclude coverage for loss exposures that typical insureds do not face. These exclusions eliminate the possibility that all insureds would have to share the costs of covering substantial loss exposures of relatively few insureds. For example, a policy might exclude coverage for destruction of a motorboat, because many insureds do not own motorboats. Watercraft policies or endorsements can provide coverage for this loss exposure.
- Eliminate coverages requiring special treatment—These coverages might require rating, underwriting, risk control, or other treatment that differs from that normally applied to the policy. An example is workers compensation coverage, which is normally provided in a self-contained policy.
- Assist in keeping premiums reasonable—Exclusions allow insurers to decline loss exposures that would increase overall insurance costs. By excluding such loss exposures, insurers can offer less costly premiums.

Exclusions typically appear in the exclusions section of the policy, but they may be contained in other policy sections, such as insuring agreements or definitions.

## Miscellaneous Provisions

Insurance policies often contain miscellaneous provisions that do not qualify strictly as declarations, definitions, insuring agreements, conditions, or exclusions. Miscellaneous provisions may deal with the relationship between the insured and the insurer or may help establish procedures for implementing the policy. Miscellaneous provisions may affect coverage but do not have the force of conditions. Consequently, if the insured does not follow procedures specified in miscellaneous provisions, the insurer typically still must fulfill its contractual promises.

### *Apply Your Knowledge*

Carol, an insurance agent, is analyzing an insurance policy that contains this provision:

We cover (a) the dwelling on the "residence premises" shown in the declarations, including structures attached to the dwelling; and (b) materials and supplies located on or next to the "residence premises" used to construct, alter or repair the dwelling or other structures on the "residence premises".

This provision is best described as which of these?

a. Declarations

b. Insuring agreement

c. Condition

d. Miscellaneous provision

*Feedback: b.* The provision is an insuring agreement because it states that the insurer will cover the described types of property.

# POLICY ANALYSIS

Each pre-loss question posed or post-loss claim filed by an insured is a unique situation that may require the analysis of policy provisions.

A common goal in analyzing an insurance policy is determining the answers to these two questions:

- Does the policy cover the loss?
- What dollar amount will the insurer pay?

Policy analysis is most efficient when the questions are considered sequentially.

## Does the Policy Cover the Loss?

Verifying policy coverage can take place either before a loss (pre-loss) or after a loss (post-loss). Pre-loss determinations, which can be difficult, usually arise in response to "what-if" questions from an applicant for insurance or an insured. A common method of policy analysis is the DICE method, which is a systematic review of all the categories of property-casualty policy provisions. See the exhibit "DICE Decision Tree."

The DICE acronym represents four of the six sections of a property-casualty insurance policy: declarations, insuring agreement, conditions, and exclusions. The other two sections of a policy are definitions and miscellaneous provisions. While the DICE acronym represents only four of the six categories of policy provisions, all six categories are analyzed in this method.

## DICE Decision Tree

To determine whether a policy covers a loss, many insurance professionals apply the DICE method. ("DICE" is an acronym for categories of policy provisions: declarations, insuring agreement, conditions, and exclusions.) The DICE method has four steps:

1. Review of the declarations page to determine whether it covers the person or the property at the time of the loss
2. Review of the insuring agreement to determine whether it covers the loss
3. Review of policy conditions to determine compliance
4. Review of policy exclusions to determine whether they preclude coverage of the loss

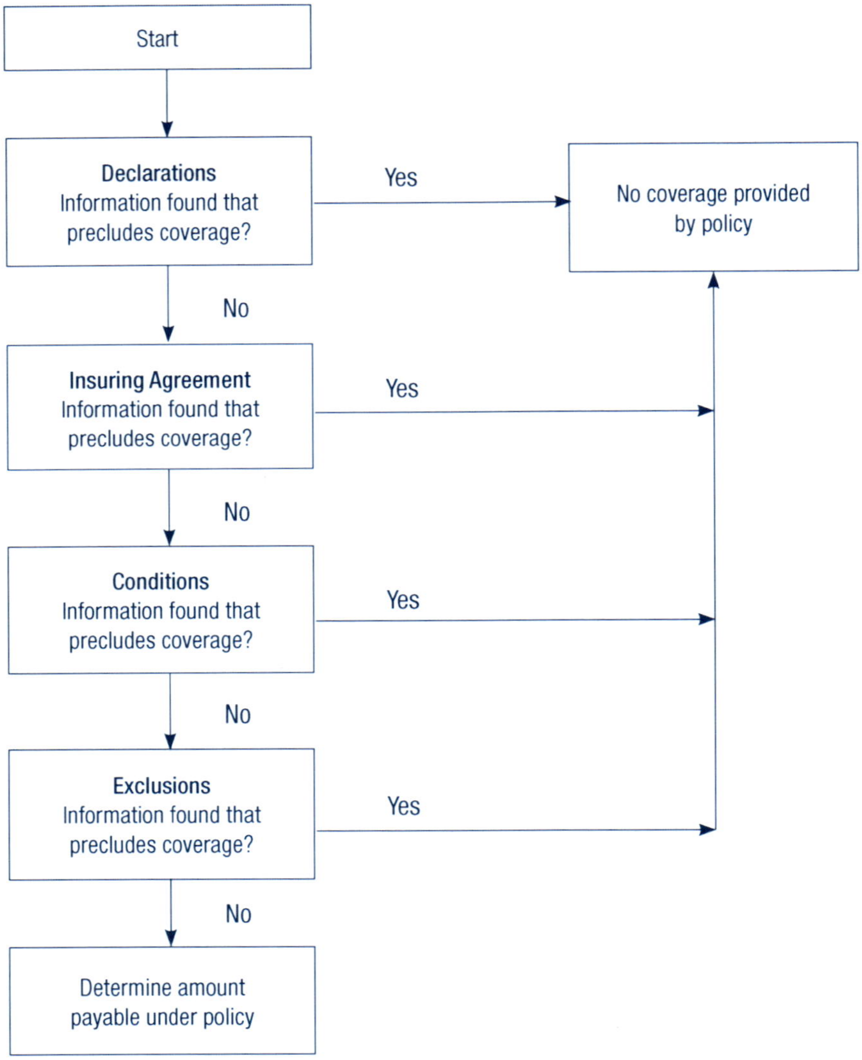


Each of these four steps is used in every case. Other categories of policy provisions should be examined. For example, endorsements and terms defined in the policy should be reviewed in relation to the declarations, insuring agreement, exclusions, and conditions.

[DA00232]

Declarations—Review of the declarations page can verify whether any information, such as policy inception and expiration dates, precludes coverage. If not, the analysis moves on to the insuring agreement.

Insuring agreement—The insuring agreement often contains provisions regarding covered property or events, covered causes of loss, and coverage territories. Analyzing definitions is also part of this step. If nothing in the insuring agreement or definitions precludes coverage, the analysis proceeds to the policy conditions.

Conditions—Policy conditions specify the duties of the insurer and insured. Failure to fulfill a condition can preclude coverage of an otherwise-covered claim. For example, a common condition requires the insured to provide timely notice of a loss to the insurer. If all conditions have been fulfilled, the analysis continues to the policy's exclusions.

Exclusions—Exclusions can appear anywhere in the policy, as well as in the policy's exclusions section; therefore, analysis of exclusions must include any categories of policy provisions that were not previously evaluated. These can include exclusions, endorsements, miscellaneous provisions, and other related documents that are part of the policy.

Although the DICE acronym represents only four of the six categories of policy provisions, the entire policy must be examined for provisions that might affect coverage. In particular, the policy definitions must be considered in the context of the provisions in which the defined terms are used, such as insuring agreements, conditions, or exclusions.

## What Dollar Amount Will the Insurer Pay?

Once it has been determined whether the loss is covered, the next task is to determine how much the insurer should pay, if so. Many insurance provisions, such as policy limits and deductibles, can affect the amount payable under a policy. Those provisions vary with the type of policy.

For property insurance, the amount payable is influenced by a policy's valuation provision, which designates whether covered property will be valued on the basis of its replacement cost, its depreciated actual cash value, or some other basis. Additionally, a deductible might apply to the amount payable. For liability insurance, the courts or a negotiated settlement can determine the amount payable.

Other applicable insurance can also affect the amounts payable for both property and liability losses. For example, a policyholder might be insured for a liability loss under two policies. If the provisions in both policies agree that the policies will share the loss in equal shares, then each policy will pay less than if there had been no other insurance.

## SUMMARY

Depending on customers' coverage needs, insurers may use either preprinted or manuscript forms to assemble insurance policies, and policies may be either self-contained or modular. Various documents may either be attached to the policy (such as an endorsement) or be incorporated by reference (such as statutory provisions).

Policy provisions communicate the terms of an insurer's and an insured's agreements as to coverage. They fall within six categories: declarations, definitions, insuring agreements, conditions, exclusions, and miscellaneous provisions.

Analyzing an insurance policy involves determining whether the policy covers a loss and, if so, what dollar amount the insurer will pay. To determine whether the policy covers a loss, the policy analyst can use the DICE method of policy analysis. Determining what dollar amount the insurer will pay requires analysis of policy provisions, such as policy limits and deductibles.

# Direct Your Learning

# 7

## Personal Insurance

### Educational Objectives

After learning the content of this assignment, you should be able to:

- Identify the common property and liability loss exposures of individuals and families.
- Given a description of a personal loss exposure or loss, determine whether it would likely be covered by any of the following coverages of a homeowners policy:
  - Dwelling
  - Other Structures
  - Personal Property
  - Loss of Use
  - Personal Liability
  - Medical Payments to Others
- Given a description of a personal loss exposure or loss, determine whether it would likely be covered by any of the following coverages of a personal auto policy:
  - Liability
  - Medical payments
  - Uninsured motorists/underinsured motorists
  - Physical damage
  - Personal injury protection
- Given a description of an individual's or a family's loss exposures, recommend one or more of the following types of personal insurance policies:
  - Dwelling policies
  - Personal umbrella policies
  - Flood policies

### Outline

# Personal Insurance

# 7

## PERSONAL LOSS EXPOSURES: PROPERTY AND LIABILITY

Before deciding what personal insurance they need, individuals and families must identify their loss exposures.

All individuals and families face loss exposures. Personal loss exposures, which include property and liability loss exposures, typically arise from the property that individuals and families own, such as homes, contents of homes, and the ownership and operation of automobiles.

### Property Loss Exposures

A **property loss exposure** exists when property can be destroyed, damaged, stolen, lost, or otherwise suffer a decrease in value because of a particular **cause of loss (peril)**. Fire is one example of a peril; theft and burglary are others.

Two types of property that are exposed to loss are **real property** and **personal property**. Examples of real property are land, crops and trees on the land, and buildings. Personal property includes the contents of a dwelling (for example, furniture, appliances, and clothing); highly valued property (for example, jewelry, silverware, firearms, and artwork); and even property such as autos, trailers, and watercraft.

Examples of property loss exposures include these:

- Fire damage to a house
- Hail damage requiring replacement of a home's roof shingles
- Wind damage to a fence surrounding a built-in swimming pool
- Water damage to the contents of a home caused by a burst pipe
- Theft of personal property
- Collision damage to an automobile
- Total loss of a sailboat that breaks loose from its moorings during a storm and sinks

Property loss exposure

A condition that presents the possibility that a person or an organization will sustain a loss resulting from damage (including destruction, taking, or loss of use) to property in which that person or organization has a financial interest.

Cause of loss (peril)

The actual means by which property is damaged or destroyed.

Real property (realty)

Tangible property consisting of land, all structures permanently attached to the land, and whatever is growing on the land.

Personal property

All tangible or intangible property that is not real property.

## Liability Loss Exposures

Liability loss exposure

Any condition or situation that presents the possibility of a claim alleging legal responsibility of a person or business for injury or damage suffered by another party.

Personal **liability loss exposures** typically arise from an individual or a family's ownership of property or from their actions. For example, anything on an individual's property that presents the possibility of someone's tripping and falling, such as uneven pavement or an exposed tree stump, is a liability loss exposure. Other common liability loss exposures associated with real property include an improperly fenced swimming pool or a secondary home occupied by tenants.

An example of a common liability loss exposure arising from personal property ownership is possession of a dog known to bite. Additionally, an individual can be sued and held liable for property damage or bodily injury caused by an automobile collision. Also, liability loss exposures can arise from the operation of a boat and can include such incidents as collision with other watercraft or bodily injury to another boater.

Personal liability loss exposures also can arise from an individual's or a family's actions. Any such actions that cause bodily injury to another party or damage to someone else's property can constitute a liability loss exposure. For example, a child could throw a rock through a neighbor's window or break a car window while playing baseball in the street.

The primary manner in which property owners treat loss exposures is by purchasing insurance. Insurance addresses most of the property and liability loss exposures that can arise as a consequence of home ownership or ownership of personal property.

---

### *Apply Your Knowledge*

Eric and Sheila own a home with a large yard and mature trees, a swimming pool, and playground equipment for the children. Sheila is a collector, and among her prized possessions are an antique dining table and chairs, a baby grand piano, and a Ming vase. Eric collects stamps and guns. Which of the following are most likely to constitute personal liability loss exposures?

a. The Ming vase
b. The playground equipment
c. The gun collection
d. The stamp collection
e. The piano

*Feedback: b. and c.* The playground equipment and the gun collection are most likely to constitute personal liability loss exposures. Injuries to children playing on the playground equipment could lead to lawsuits against Eric and Sheila. Even though Eric is keeping the guns as part of a collection, if one of his children or a guest loads and handles one of the firearms, it could discharge and cause injury or death, resulting in a lawsuit against Eric and Sheila.

---

# THE HOMEOWNERS POLICY

A homeowners policy contains coverage for the real property, personal property, and personal liability loss exposures that arise as a consequence of homeownership.

Under a typical Insurance Services Office (ISO) homeowners policy, there is a declarations page that provides details about the insured and the policy coverage. Property coverages are found under Section I, and liability coverages are found under Section II. Each section contains insuring agreements, policy conditions, and exclusions.

## Section I—Property Coverages

Section I of an ISO homeowners policy provides these primary coverages:

- Dwelling
- Other Structures
- Personal Property
- Loss of Use

Dwelling coverage provides insurance for the insured's dwelling (the house itself). Coverage also extends to any structures attached to the house, such as an attached garage or carport. A homeowners policy can provide protection against various types of loss exposures, such as fire damage to the dwelling, wind damage to the roof, or smoke damage to the kitchen walls.

Other structures coverage provides insurance for various detached structures that are located on the residence premises. Structures that are not attached to the dwelling are also covered by a homeowners policy. Other structures must be separated from the dwelling by a clear space or have only an incidental connection to the dwelling, such as a utility line, walkway, or fence. Examples of other structures include sheds, detached garages, and swimming pools. A homeowners insurance policy can protect against loss exposures such as fire damage to a detached garage, lightning damage to a swimming pool, or fire damage to a fence.

Personal property coverage provides protection for the insured's property other than the dwelling and other structures. Examples of personal property include furniture, appliances, and clothing. A homeowners policy can provide protection against loss exposures such as water damage to rugs from a pipe bursting, fire damage to furniture, or theft of jewelry.

Loss of use coverage insures financial losses that result when part or all of an insured residence is rendered uninhabitable by a covered loss. For example, a residence with significant fire damage may not be fit for occupancy while it is being repaired. A kitchen fire may make the kitchen and dining area of a residence unusable. One of the benefits of loss of use coverage is reimbursement to the insured for living or meal expenses during the period of repairs.

Fair rental value

Under Coverage D—Loss of Use of a homeowners policy, the amount of rent (less any discontinued expenses) that the insured would have received for the residence or any part of the residence rented to another individual for residential purposes, if the residence had not been damaged.

Liability

A legal responsibility for the consequences of an act or omission.

Another benefit is coverage for **fair rental value** of the damaged property if the portion of the home that was damaged (eligible under a homeowners form) was rented to a tenant.

## Section II—Liability Coverages

Section II of a homeowners policy provides these **liability** coverages:

- Personal Liability
- Medical Payments to Others

Personal liability coverage provides insurance for claims for bodily injury or property damage for which the insured is legally liable. Personal liability coverage is usually purchased with a limit of liability of $300,000 or more. The limit applies to each occurrence, and the insurer has an obligation to defend the insured and the right to conduct an investigation. Examples of liability claims against homeowners include injuries sustained in a fall on a homeowner's property or damage to a neighbor's property from a fire that starts in a homeowner's unattended barbecue grill.

Medical payments to others coverage provides payment for medical expenses to persons other than the insured as a result of an accident at the insured's premises. The insured does not have to be liable for the accident, and the claim must be made within three years of the occurrence. For example, if a guest cuts her finger on a kitchen knife while assisting the insured and requires stitches, coverage for the medical costs would be available up to the coverage limit. Typically, limits for medical payments to others coverage are much lower than for liability coverage, usually $5,000 or less.

## Choice of Policy Forms and Covered Perils

ISO offers individuals and families a choice of policy forms to meet their particular needs. The forms differ in the types of property and perils covered under Section I. See the exhibit "Homeowners Policy Forms and Covered Perils."

Named peril

A specific cause of loss listed and described in an insurance policy. Also used to describe policies containing named perils.

Open perils

A type of policy or coverage that insures against risks of direct physical loss except for those specifically excluded or limited by the policy.

ISO homeowners policies all follow a similar pattern and include declarations, Section I, and Section II. However, the policy forms vary in coverage specifics. For example, a Broad Form (HO-2) covers the dwelling and other structures as well as personal property on a **named perils** basis. The Special Form (HO-3) provides coverage for the dwelling and other structures on an **open perils** basis but covers personal property on a named perils basis.

## Homeowners Policy Forms and Covered Perils

| Policy Form | Coverage Provided | Covered Perils |
|---|---|---|
| HO-2<br>Broad Form | This form provides coverage for owner-occupants of dwellings. It provides Section I coverages on a named perils basis and provides Section II coverage. | Fire or lightning; windstorm or hail; explosion; riot or civil commotion; aircraft; vehicles; smoke; vandalism or malicious mischief; theft; volcanic eruption |
| HO-3<br>Special Form | This form provides coverage for owner-occupants of dwellings. It insures the dwelling and other structures on an open perils basis and personal property on a named perils basis. Section II coverage is also provided. | For dwelling and other structures: open perils. For personal property: Broad Form covered perils, plus: falling objects; weight of ice, snow, or sleet; accidental discharge or overflow of water or steam; sudden and accidental tearing apart; cracking, burning, or bulging; freezing; sudden and accidental damage from artificially generated electrical current |
| HO-4<br>Contents Broad Form | This form is designed for tenants and other occupants of dwellings or apartments. It insures a tenant's personal property on a named perils basis (no dwelling coverage is included). Section II coverage is also provided. | Broad Form covered perils |
| HO-5<br>Comprehensive Form | This form is designed for owner-occupants of dwellings. It provides the broadest coverage of all the homeowners forms. It insures the dwelling, other structures, and personal property on an open perils basis. Loss of use and Section II coverages are also provided. | Open perils on dwelling, other structures, and personal property (loss of use coverage based on loss sustained under Coverages A, B, and C) |
| HO-6<br>Unit-Owners Form | This form is designed for the owners of residential condominium units. It insures personal property on a named perils basis, with limited dwelling coverage (unit improvements and betterments). Loss of Use and Section II coverages are also provided. | Broad Form covered perils |
| HO-8<br>Modified Coverage Form | This form is a more limited form of coverage for owner-occupants of dwellings. Insures the dwelling, other structures, and personal property, on a limited, named perils basis. | Fire or lightning, windstorm or hail, explosion, riot or civil commotion, aircraft, vehicles, smoke, vandalism or malicious mischief, theft, volcanic eruption |

[DA00460]

## *Apply Your Knowledge*

Brad and Carol are insured under a homeowners policy that includes theft as a covered cause of loss. A burglar broke into their garage (which is not attached to their house) and stole their lawnmower and some power tools. The cost of replacing the stolen items would likely be covered under which one of the following coverages in Brad and Carol's homeowners policy?

a. Dwelling

b. Other Structures

c. Personal Property

d. Loss of Use

*Feedback*: c. Although the property was stolen from an "other structure," the type of property stolen was "personal property."

# THE PERSONAL AUTO POLICY

An individual or a family can use a personal auto policy (PAP) to insure an auto against the consequences of losses such as an auto being struck by an at-fault driver (as a collision, or property loss) or an insured auto striking and damaging another vehicle (as a liability loss). A PAP can also cover medical expenses, loss of income, and even funeral expenses incurred by the insured or the insured's family members as a result of being injured in an auto accident.

Under a typical PAP, insureds can select from a number of coverage options to address the various loss exposures that may arise from their ownership or operation of an auto, including these:

- Liability coverage
- Medical payments coverage
- Uninsured motorists coverage/underinsured motorists coverage
- Physical damage coverage
- Personal injury protection

PAP liability coverage corresponds to liability exposures, and PAP physical damage coverage corresponds to property exposures. Medical payments coverage, uninsured motorists coverage, and personal injury protection coverage (which can be added to the PAP by endorsement) cover losses resulting from bodily injury to the insured and family members.

Auto policies also have a declarations page that contains details about the policy coverage. Coverage is further influenced by related policy conditions and exclusions, and additional coverages can be attached by endorsement.

## Liability Coverage

PAP liability coverage protects an insured against a claim or lawsuit for bodily injury to pedestrians, occupants of the insured's car, and occupants of other autos, and for property damage to others caused by an insured as a consequence of an auto accident. In order for the liability portion of the policy to pay, the insured must be found legally responsible for the accident.

A typical loss covered under PAP liability coverage would be injuries to a pedestrian who, while legally crossing the street, is struck by a vehicle driven by the insured. Similarly, if an insured driver strikes another vehicle at a traffic light, any damage to the other vehicle would be covered by the insured's PAP liability coverage.

Liability coverage applies to vehicles described in the declarations and also applies, for example, to insureds while they are driving a neighbor's auto or if they rent a car while on vacation. A PAP is intended to cover only occasional use of a nonowned auto. It does not cover insureds while they are driving other cars that are furnished to them or made available for their regular use. For example, a PAP would not cover losses caused by an insured in a pickup truck his employer provides for his regular use. See the exhibit "Miscellaneous Vehicles Endorsement."

### Miscellaneous Vehicles Endorsement

One common type of endorsement modifies a PAP to cover personal vehicles other than regular autos, such as motorcycles, snowmobiles, all-terrain vehicles, and campers—often referred to as recreational or miscellaneous vehicles. Some insurers that specialize in recreational or miscellaneous vehicles develop special policies for covering such vehicles.

[DA07478]

A PAP also provides coverage to other people who occasionally drive one of the insured's cars. For example, if a neighbor borrowed the insured's auto, the insured's PAP would cover the neighbor's use of this vehicle. Should an accident occur that is the neighbor's fault, the liability portion of the insured's policy would respond.

## Medical Payments Coverage

PAP medical payments coverage pays for the reasonable and necessary medical expenses an insured incurs because of bodily injury caused by an auto accident.

Coverage is provided for bodily injury to occupants of the insured's auto if they sustain injuries as the result of an auto accident or while they are entering or exiting the insured's auto. Coverage also applies to an insured who, as a pedestrian, is struck by another vehicle.

Medical payments coverage is paid without regard to whether the insured is at fault. For example, an insured may be driving an auto that is struck by another vehicle whose driver has ignored a traffic signal. Although the other driver is at fault, the insured can be compensated for any injuries sustained as a consequence of the accident under the insured's PAP medical payments coverage.

Medical payments coverage is payable subject to a per-person limit that is usually set for an amount (such as $5,000) that is much lower than the amount of insurance for liability coverage (such as $300,000).

## Uninsured Motorists Coverage/Underinsured Motorists Coverage

Uninsured motorists (UM) coverage

Coverage that provides a source of recovery for occupants of a covered auto or for qualifying pedestrians who are injured in an accident caused by an at-fault motorist who does not have the state minimum liability insurance or by a hit-and-run driver.

**Uninsured motorists coverage** (UM) pays if an insured incurs bodily injury (and in some states, property damage) caused by an at-fault uninsured motorist, including a hit-and-run driver or a driver whose insurer is insolvent. The loss exposure is any type of bodily injury sustained by the insured for the uninsured damages.

Consider a case in which the insured driver is struck by a hit-and-run driver. Further assume that the insured's car is deemed a total loss and that the insured sustains injuries of more than $50,000, far in excess of the insured's medical payments limit. If the driver were known, the insured would normally attempt to obtain recovery from the at-fault driver's auto liability coverage. When an insured has a legal right to recover damages and a source of recovery is not available because of the consequences of the previously described loss exposures, the insured can turn to the PAP uninsured motorist coverage for compensation.

Underinsured motorists coverage

Coverage that provides compensation to insureds who have suffered bodily injury in an accident with an at-fault motorist whose bodily injury liability insurance limits are lower than the injured person's underinsured motorists coverage and are not sufficient to pay all the insured's damages.

A related coverage, **underinsured motorists coverage** (UIM) is provided as an endorsement to the PAP. It is included automatically with the PAP in some states because it operates closely with uninsured motorists coverage. Underinsured motorists coverage pays if an insured incurs bodily injury (and, in some states, property damage) caused by an underinsured motorist who is found liable in an accident involving the insured. The loss exposure is any type of bodily injury sustained by the insured for the underinsured damages. The coverage typically pays the difference between the underinsured motorists coverage limit on the insured's vehicle and the liability limits on the at-fault vehicle (up to the maximum underinsured motorists limit).

## Physical Damage Coverage

Physical damage coverage is property insurance that covers damage to, or loss of, covered autos. Coverage can apply to an insured's covered auto as well as to certain nonowned autos, less any applicable policy deductible.

Nonowned autos can include vehicles borrowed by the insured that are not available for the insured's regular use, or any auto or trailer not owned by the insured that is being used as a temporary substitute for the insured's auto because of breakdown, servicing, or destruction. For nonowned autos, coverage is excess over other collectible insurance, which means that the PAP physical damage coverage for nonowned autos begins paying only after all other collectible insurance coverages have been exhausted.

The insured can select from two types of physical damage coverage: **collision coverage** and **other than collision (OTC) coverage**. Collision coverage is an optional coverage under the PAP and is typically available only when other than collision coverage also is purchased.

Collision coverage
Coverage for direct and accidental loss or damage to a covered auto caused by collision with another object or by overturn.

Other than collision (OTC) coverage
Coverage for physical damage to a covered auto resulting from any cause of loss except collision or a cause of loss specifically excluded.

Collision coverage insures damage to a covered auto resulting from the auto's striking an object or another auto, or from the auto's upset. Upset occurs when a vehicle overturns or loses its equilibrium. Collision loss exposures can include vehicle upset as a consequence of operation; collision with another auto; or collision with an object, such as a guardrail or building.

Other than collision coverage applies to losses that do not fall within the policy's definition of collision. Auto policies typically do not define what constitutes an other than collision loss. If a loss is not considered collision, then it usually is considered other than collision. Because the coverage is so broad, many insurance practitioners refer to the coverage as comprehensive physical damage coverage.

A PAP lists causes of loss that the policy considers other than collision. These causes of loss include fire, theft, animal contact, flood, and glass breakage. Other than collision loss exposures can consequently include auto theft, water damage due to flood, contact with an animal, or fire damage. See the exhibit "Other Than Collision Coverage Example."

### Other Than Collision Coverage Example

Linda has just purchased a new sedan. On her way home from the new car dealer, she inadvertently strikes a deer on a rural road, causing $4,500 of damage to the car. When Linda purchased the car, she requested a PAP with a $500 other than collision deductible and a $1,000 collision deductible from her insurance agent. The deer strike is covered under the PAP and is considered an other than collision loss, so Linda will receive a $4,000 payment from her insurer.

($4,500 – $500 deductible = $4,000 payment.)

[DA07479]

## Personal Injury Protection

Many states have enacted laws that allow individuals injured in auto accidents to collect payment for damages from their own insurers regardless of

**No-fault automobile insurance**

Insurance that covers automobile accident victims on a first-party basis, allowing them to collect damages from their own insurers regardless of who was at fault.

**Personal injury protection (PIP) coverage**

Coverage that pays benefits, regardless of fault, for medical expense, income loss, and other benefits, resulting from bodily injury to occupants of a covered auto.

who is at fault. These laws authorize or mandate **no-fault automobile insurance**—often referred to as **personal injury protection (PIP)**—and define the benefits that insurers can or must provide.

No-fault laws vary significantly from state to state. True no-fault laws restrict a victim's right to sue a negligent driver. For example, if claims resulting from an accident are below a threshold—which may be a dollar amount or may be based on other criteria, such as seriousness of injuries—victims can collect only from their own insurers. If claims exceed the specified threshold, the victims can file a liability claim or sue the negligent driver for damages resulting from the accident.

Insureds can obtain PIP coverage by adding an endorsement to their auto insurance policy. PIP endorsements vary by state; in some states, the no-fault laws specify precise policy language to be used in the endorsement.

---

### *Apply Your Knowledge*

Driving late one night, Jeff failed to notice a stop sign, pulled into an intersection, and struck another auto. Jeff was unhurt, but the other driver was seriously injured. Both autos sustained significant physical damage, and Jeff was held to be legally responsible for the accident. Which one of the following combinations of coverages from Jeff's PAP would apply to this accident?

a. Liability coverage and medical payments coverage

b. Medical payments coverage and uninsured motorists coverage

c. Liability coverage and physical damage coverage

d. Uninsured motorists coverage and physical damage coverage

*Feedback: c.* Liability coverage and physical damage coverage under Jeff's PAP would apply to this accident. Liability coverage would pay for the other driver's medical expenses, lost income, and auto damage. Physical damage coverage would pay for the damage to Jeff's car.

---

# OTHER PERSONAL INSURANCE POLICIES

Personal auto policies and homeowners policies adequately address many loss exposures that affect individuals and families. Some loss exposures, however, require additional coverage.

Other personal insurance policies are available to meet a variety of personal insurance needs and to protect insureds against certain loss exposures arising from property ownership and nonbusiness activities. Three common types of additional personal insurance policies are these:

- Dwelling policies
- Personal umbrella policies
- Flood policies

## Dwelling Policies

Although a homeowners policy covers most owner-occupied homes, many dwellings do not meet the eligibility requirements for a homeowners policy. For example, a dwelling might not be owner-occupied, or it might be a four-family building in a state where only one- and two-family dwellings are eligible for homeowners coverage. In such cases, the dwelling and its contents can generally be insured under a dwelling policy.

Dwelling policy coverage is more limited and narrower in scope than that provided by homeowners policies. Dwelling policies typically provide coverage for the dwelling, other structures, and personal property. They also provide fair rental value coverage. Personal liability coverage is not included in dwelling policies, and coverage for liability must be added by endorsement, for additional premium, if the insured would like to include liability coverage in the dwelling policy. An insured who lives elsewhere in a primary home and rents the dwelling may be able to extend personal liability coverage from his or her primary homeowners policy to the rental property.

Dwelling policies provide property coverage (and liability coverage when added by endorsement) for loss exposures that arise as a consequence of dwelling ownership. For example, typical covered loss exposures include fire damage to the dwelling or wind damage to its roof. If liability coverage is added by endorsement, certain injuries arising from the insured's negligence in maintaining the property would also be covered.

## Personal Umbrella Policies

Personal umbrella insurance, or an **umbrella policy**, is a generic term for a broad liability policy intended to provide high liability limits in excess of basic liability policy coverage. Umbrella policies usually have a liability limit of $1 million or more, which is added to the liability limits of an insured's other policies, such as a personal auto policy or a homeowners policy.

Umbrella policy

A liability policy that provides excess coverage above underlying policies and may also provide coverage not available in the underlying policies, subject to a self-insured retention.

If, for example, a catastrophic auto accident occurs and losses for bodily injury and property damage exceed an insured's auto liability limit, the insured's umbrella policy would pay the excess of the loss up to its limit of liability. As another example, assume an individual who trips and falls on an insured's sidewalk subsequently sues the insured and the judgment is for $500,000 against the insured. The insured's homeowners policy would provide coverage up to its limit (referred to as the "underlying" limit), and the umbrella policy would pay the excess to bring the total to $500,000. See the exhibit "Personal Umbrella Policy."

## Personal Umbrella Policy

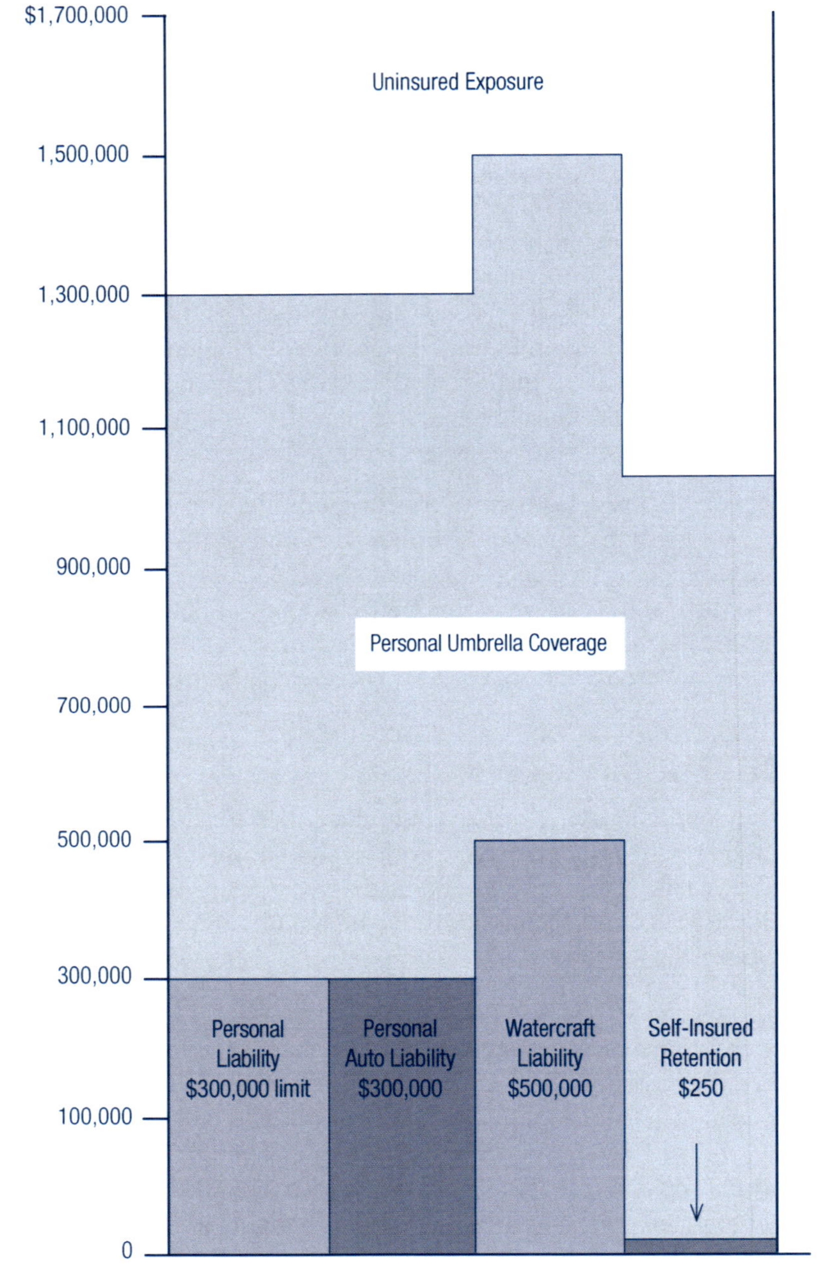


[DA00463]

## Flood Policies

A flood is a rising or an overflowing of water onto what is normally dry land. Coverage for the peril of flood is excluded by homeowners policies, dwelling policies, and most other insurance policies that cover property at a fixed location. Flood damage is, however, covered under most auto policies that include physical damage coverage.

Some floods cause widespread, catastrophic damage that would create unmanageably large losses for a private insurer that had issued many property policies in the flood area. Therefore, the federal government provides flood insurance through two mechanisms. Insurance can be obtained directly through the National Flood Insurance Program, or a producer can place the business with an insurer that participates in the Federal Insurance Administration's "Write Your Own" program. Eligibility requirements apply to flood insurance's individual building and contents coverage. Communities also must meet eligibility requirements to qualify for the "regular" flood program, which offers better rates and higher building and contents limits than those available in the "emergency" program.

Flood insurance provides property coverage (building and contents) for certain loss exposures that arise as a consequence of property ownership in flood hazard areas. Loss exposures covered under a flood policy include the consequence of flood damage to an insured's building after a river overflows its banks, or destruction of a building's contents if a flood from the same overflowing river sweeps the building and its contents away. An eligible applicant for a single-family dwelling in a community eligible for the "regular" flood program may be able to obtain the flood program maximum limits of $250,000 building coverage and $100,000 maximum contents coverage for the dwelling.

---

### *Apply Your Knowledge*

The Morley family has just purchased a large property. They entertain frequently and plan to invite friends to stay in their home. The liability limit in their homeowners policy is $300,000. Which personal insurance policy would you recommend for the Morleys?

a. Flood insurance policy

b. Dwelling policy

c. Umbrella policy

d. Personal auto policy

*Feedback:* c. Because the Morleys entertain frequently and have guests stay in their home, an umbrella policy would be recommended to provide additional liability coverage.

---

# SUMMARY

Personal loss exposures, which typically arise as a consequence of owning property, are of two types. Personal property loss exposures exist when property can be destroyed, damaged, stolen, or lost or can otherwise decrease in value because of a specific cause of loss. Liability loss exposures arise from the possibility that an individual or a family member may be legally responsible for injuries or property damage sustained by others. Insurance addresses most personal property and liability loss exposures.

The primary manner in which individuals and families treat the majority of property and liability loss exposures that arise as a consequence of owning property is by purchasing insurance.

Various types of ISO homeowners policies are available to meet the particular needs of individuals and families. All of these policies contain declarations, Section I—Property Coverages, and Section II—Liability Coverages, with differences in the specific types of property and perils covered under each form.

A personal auto policy (PAP) combines property insurance coverage and liability insurance coverage in a single policy. A typical personal auto policy allows insureds to select from among various coverages, including liability, medical payments, uninsured/underinsured motorists, physical damage, and personal injury protection (PIP) to address their various property and liability loss exposures.

Many individuals and families require additional types of insurance coverage besides their homeowners and personal auto policies to address their various loss exposures. These additional personal insurance policies include dwelling policies, personal umbrella policies, and flood policies.

Direct Your Learning

8

# Commercial Property Insurance

## Educational Objectives

After learning the content of this assignment, you should be able to:

- Identify the common property loss exposures of commercial insureds in terms of the following:
  - Types of property
  - Causes of loss
  - Financial consequences
- Given a description of a commercial loss exposure or a loss, determine whether it would likely be covered by any of the following:
  - A commercial property policy, such as the Building and Personal Property Coverage Form with Basic Form, Broad Form, or Special Form coverage
  - Inland marine insurance
  - Business income and/or extra expense insurance

## Outline

# Commercial Property Insurance

# 8

## COMMERCIAL PROPERTY LOSS EXPOSURES

Commercial property loss exposures can be identified in terms of types of property, causes of loss, and financial consequences.

A business that sustains major damage to its building experiences consequences that extend beyond the building itself. For example, owners of a retail store damaged by fire would incur the costs of rebuilding the damaged structure, as well as expenses related to the loss of the building's contents, cleanup costs, fire department charges, and income lost while the store is closed. Additional expenditures may be required to reestablish the business.

All of these considerations relate to components of a property loss exposure. Insurance professionals often identify property loss exposures in terms of these three elements:

- The types of property that might be exposed to loss, damage, or destruction
- The causes of loss that might lead to loss, damage, or destruction of property
- The financial consequences of a property loss

For example, an insurance professional might speak of a building exposure (type of property), a windstorm exposure (cause of loss), or a loss of business income exposure (financial consequence). Similarly, a property loss exposure could be identified more specifically in terms of two or even all three of these elements, such as a building fire exposure or loss of business income resulting from windstorm damage to a building and its contents.

### Types of Property

Property is any item with value. Individuals, families, and organizations own and use property, depend on it as a source of income or services, and rely on its value. Property can decline in value—or even become worthless—if it is lost, damaged, or destroyed.

Any item of property can be classified as either real property or personal property. It is important for a business owner to consider all property loss exposures that could affect the business, even if some of them (such as land) typically are uninsurable.

Real property is tangible property consisting of land, all structures permanently attached to the land, and whatever is growing on the land. Examples of real property, in addition to land, are buildings, driveways, sidewalks, underground piping, and radio transmission towers. All property that is not real property is personal property. Examples of personal property include vehicles, merchandise, furniture, tools, and clothing.

For insurance purposes, it is useful to categorize real and personal property into these classifications:

- Buildings
- Contents
- Property in transit
- Property in the possession of others
- Floating property

## Buildings

A building consists of more than walls and a roof. Most buildings also include plumbing, wiring, and heating and air conditioning equipment. A high-rise building usually has elevators and may have specially designed platforms, hoists, and tracks used by window washers. Such equipment is also considered part of the building. Items permanently attached to the structure, such as built-in appliances, also are considered part of the building.

## Contents

Contents

Personal property that is usually contained in a building or other structure.

The **contents** of a commercial building might include these items:

- Furniture, such as the desks in an office
- Machinery and equipment, such as cash registers
- Stock, such as raw materials and completed products in inventory

Although most insurance policies use the term "personal property" to refer to the contents of a building, many insurance practitioners and policyholders use the term "contents" as a matter of convenience and common practice.

Property insurance policies typically refer to personal property, rather than contents, because the property often is covered even when it is not literally contained in the building. Commercial property policies generally use the term "business personal property."

## Property in Transit

Most businesses ship property (such as merchandise) to others or receive property (such as raw materials or supplies) from others. Property in transit may be transported by truck, railcar, airplane, watercraft, or even by bicycle or on foot. A shipment may be sent to a client's office a few blocks away, to a buyer on the other side of the world, or anywhere in between. Property in transit

▶▶

may be transported on the owner's own vehicles or by a transportation company. The property may be in transit for a few minutes or for several months. Because of all these variables, many insurance policies covering buildings and contents exclude property in transit. A firm that wishes to insure its property in transit must usually purchase separate cargo insurance.

### Property in the Possession of Others

In many situations, an organization may place its property in the temporary possession of others for processing, cleaning, repair, adjustment, storage, exhibition, or sale. Because the probability of loss at the temporary location could differ greatly from the probability of loss at the owner's location, building and contents insurance policies usually provide only a nominal amount of insurance for property at other locations.

Like property in transit, property in the possession of others can be insured for its full value under specialized policies designed for that purpose.

### Floating Property

Many businesses own property that normally is situated at ever-changing work sites or in transit between work sites. Examples of this kind of property include a wedding photographer's cameras and a building contractor's tools and mobile equipment. Such property is often referred to as "floating property" because it does not remain at a single location for a sustained period. Insurance for such property is available under specialized inland marine policies called "floaters."

## Causes of Loss to Property

The potential causes of loss to property are another important aspect of property loss exposures. A cause of loss adversely affects property and leaves it in an altered state. For example, a fire can reduce a building to a heap of rubble. Vandalism can damage a building or its contents. Some causes of loss do not alter the property itself but do affect a person's ability to possess or use the property. For example, property lost or stolen may still be used, but not by its rightful owner.

Buildings and personal property are subject to many potential causes of loss. Some of the most significant perils include fire, theft, windstorm, flood, earthquake, terrorism, and war.

For most insureds, fire is the peril that poses the greatest risk of a large or even total property loss. Hurricanes and tornadoes are both examples of windstorms, although less violent windstorms also can cause property damage. Windstorms pose a catastrophic exposure for insurers and insureds in areas exposed to hurricanes. For instance, in 2005, Hurricane Katrina caused more than $41 billion in insured losses (2005 dollars), while four hurricanes that struck Florida and other areas of the United States in 2004 caused $22 billion (2004 dollars) in insured losses.[1]

Similarly, flood, earthquake, terrorism, and war pose catastrophic exposures. For example, insured property losses at the World Trade Center and Pentagon from the terrorist attacks of September 11, 2001, have been estimated to exceed $18 billion.[2]

## Financial Consequences of Property Losses

Financial consequences are the third and final important aspect of property loss exposures. The adverse financial consequences of a property loss may include a reduction in the value of the property, lost income, and/or extra expenses.

### Property Value Reduction

When a property loss occurs, the property's value is reduced. This reduction in value can be measured in different ways. Property that must be replaced has no remaining worth, unless some salvageable items can be sold. If the property can be repaired or restored, the reduction in value can be measured by the cost of the repair or restoration. For example, if a fence worth $7,000 is damaged by a falling tree and the fence owner has to pay $2,000 to have the damage repaired, the fence owner has incurred a partial loss that reduces the value of the fence by $2,000.

### Lost Income

A business may lose income as a result of a property loss. When property is damaged, income might be lost because the property cannot be used until it has been repaired, restored, or replaced. For example, when a business suffers a serious fire, it might have to close until repairs to the building are made and personal property is replaced. The resulting loss of income occurs over time.

As another example, the owner of a rental property faces rental income loss if the property is damaged and temporarily unavailable for rent. The owner would probably continue to incur some expenses, such as mortgage payments and taxes, but would not receive the rent that helped pay those expenses.

Determining the amount of business income that might be lost because of a property loss requires estimating an organization's future level of activity and performing a "what if" analysis that asks, "What if the business could not operate for six months because it would take six months to rebuild after a fire? How much income would be lost?"

### Extra Expenses

For a business to determine the extent of a property loss exposure, it must consider the extra expenses that the loss of the property would require.

When property is damaged, the property itself declines in value, and the owner or other affected party suffers a corresponding loss. In addition, the owner or other user of that property might incur extra expenses in acquiring a temporary substitute or in temporarily maintaining the damaged property in a usable condition. Consider these examples:

- When a store's premises are damaged, the owners might have to rent temporary space at considerably greater expense than their normal rent.
- When a newspaper company's printing presses are damaged, the company might spend extra money to print the newspaper on another newspaper company's presses.
- When a bank building is damaged, the bank might hire additional guards until the building can be made secure.

# COMMERCIAL PROPERTY COVERAGES

To ensure their business can survive accidental property loss, prudent business owners should identify their property loss exposures and insure themselves against the financial consequences of damage from fire and other causes of property loss.

Insurance professionals should assist business owners in determining whether the commercial property insurance they purchase will restore the financial condition of their business to its pre-loss state in the event of a significant loss. To do so, insurance professionals should be familiar with the provisions of property insurance policies and assist business owners in understanding these elements:

- Covered property
- Covered locations
- Covered causes of loss
- Covered financial consequences, such as loss of business income

## Covered Property

A property insurance policy specifies the property that it covers by identifying it with a broad description and then refining that description through a series of limitations and exclusions. The **Building and Personal Property Coverage Form (BPP)** is often used to insure buildings, the insured's business personal property, and the personal property of others. The insured can buy coverage for any combination of these three categories.

**Building and Personal Property Coverage Form (BPP)**
A commercial property coverage form that can be used to cover buildings, "your business personal property," and personal property of others.

However, the BPP and similar commercial property forms exclude coverage for certain types of structures, such as bridges, and certain types of business personal property, such as money and securities. Moreover, the BPP and similar forms provide limited coverage for property away from the insured's premises. Consequently, insurers offer additional types of property coverage, such as inland marine insurance, to cover loss exposures that are excluded by the BPP and similar forms.

## Buildings

In commercial property insurance, a permanent structure with walls and a roof is usually called a building. Other outdoor structures, such as carports, antenna towers, and swimming pools, although not considered buildings in the traditional sense, may be insured under building coverage. The BPP's definition of building also includes these kinds of property:

Fixture

Any personal property affixed to real property in such a way as to become part of the real property.

- Completed additions to covered buildings
- **Fixtures** (including outdoor fixtures)
- Permanently installed machinery and equipment
- Personal property owned by the insured and used to maintain or service the building or its premises (for example, fire extinguishing equipment; outdoor furniture; and equipment for refrigeration, ventilation, cooking, dishwashing, or laundering)

The inclusion of some items of personal property under building coverage allows a building's owner, such as a landlord, who has no other building contents to insure, to forgo purchasing separate personal property insurance. This is advantageous because the rate for building insurance is typically lower than the rate for personal property insurance.

## Business Personal Property

The BPP and other commercial property insurance policies usually refer to the contents of buildings as "business personal property." The BPP's definition of "business personal property" specifies that coverage for the insured's business personal property applies to such items as furniture, machinery, and equipment that are not part of the building; and to stock, including merchandise, raw materials, and in-process or finished goods. Coverage generally applies only when the property is located in or on the described building or in the open or a vehicle within 100 feet of the premises.

## Personal Property of Others

Coverage for personal property of others is designed to protect the insured against loss or damage to the personal property of others while such property is in the custody of the insured. This coverage is important for businesses, referred to as **bailees**, that usually have customers' property in their custody, such as laundries, dry cleaners, and appliance repair shops.

Bailee

The party temporarily possessing the personal property in a bailment.

The BPP covers the personal property of others only while the property is in the insured's care, custody, or control and in or on the building described in the policy declarations or within 100 feet of the described premises. Coverage applies regardless of whether the insured is legally responsible for the damage.

## Covered Locations

In addition to describing covered property, a commercial property insurance policy identifies where the property is covered. Identifying a covered building by its street address is appropriate because its location is fixed. In contrast, the determination of the location of covered personal property can be complicated because buildings and personal property do not necessarily remain at a fixed location. For example, the building contents might be removed from the premises for repair or storage, furniture might be found not only inside buildings but also on outdoor patios and decks, or items usually kept in a building might be temporarily located in a car or truck.

The BPP and similar policies provide coverage for property that is on or within 100 feet of the insured premises. However, most commercial property policies often include a coverage extension that provides a certain amount of coverage, such as $10,000, for property temporarily situated at other premises. This extension, however, applies only to losses that occur in the specified policy territory, typically the United States and Canada.

**Inland marine insurance** covers many loss exposures that the BPP and similar forms exclude. These exposures include property in domestic transit; property situated at the premises of others; and "floating property," such as a contractor's tools and equipment, which could be situated at several different job sites during the policy period.

Inland marine insurance

Insurance that covers many different classes of property that typically involve an element of transportation.

Policies covering floating (movable) property might have territorial limits, or might provide coverage anywhere in the world.

Insurers prefer to insure such property separately from the BPP because it gives them the opportunity to use insurance conditions and rates that are appropriate for the loss exposures being covered.

---

### *Apply Your Knowledge*

SPR Construction Company owns various pieces of mechanized equipment, such as bulldozers and backhoes, that are used at SPR's job sites. What type of insurance would be best suited for insuring this equipment against property loss at any of SPR's job sites or in transit between them?

a. The Building and Personal Property Coverage Form

b. Business income insurance

c. Extra expense insurance

d. Inland marine insurance

*Feedback: d.* Inland marine insurance covers many loss exposures that the BPP and similar forms exclude, such as "floating property," which could be situated at several different job sites during the policy period.

---

## Covered Causes of Loss

In addition to covered property and covered locations, property policy provisions also specify the covered causes of loss, or perils. These are the three different levels of coverage for commercial property policies on buildings:

- Basic Form coverage—the lowest-cost version that provides coverage for approximately one dozen named perils.
- Broad Form coverage—a higher-cost version that adds several perils to those covered by basic coverage.
- Special Form (open perils) coverage—the highest-cost version that covers all causes of loss that are not specifically excluded. Special Form coverage covers all the perils of Broad Form coverage, as well as other perils.

Property insurance policies define many causes of loss in some detail. The precise definitions vary by policy.

### Basic Form Coverage

These are the causes of loss generally included in commercial property policies that provide Basic Form coverage: fire; lightning; explosion; windstorm or hail; smoke; aircraft or vehicles; riot or civil commotion; vandalism; sprinkler leakage; sinkhole collapse; volcanic action; and fungus, wet rot, dry rot, and bacteria (provided as an additional limited coverage).

### Broad Form Coverage

Some property insurance policies add coverage against additional causes of loss and are commonly referred to as "Broad Form coverage" policies. The additional causes of loss covered under Broad Form coverage are falling objects; weight of snow, ice, or sleet; water damage; and collapse caused by certain perils (provided as an additional coverage). See the exhibit "Covered Causes of Loss in Basic and Broad Forms."

### Special Form (Open Perils) Coverage

"Special Form coverage" or "open perils" are terms that describe the coverage provided in commercial property insurance policies covering all causes of loss that are not specifically excluded. For example, the Special Form includes coverage for theft of covered property, a peril not included under the Basic and Broad Forms. Special Form coverage policies were once described as "all-risk," but this term is now less commonly used because it may be misconstrued to mean that all risks of loss are covered.

### Causes of Loss Often Excluded

Some perils that could affect a large group of people at the same time generally are considered to be commercially uninsurable because of the magnitude of potential losses. Almost all property insurance policies exclude coverage

### Covered Causes of Loss in Basic and Broad Forms

| Both Forms Cover: | Broad Form Also Covers: |
|---|---|
| Fire | Falling objects |
| Lightning | Weight of snow, ice, or sleet |
| Explosion | Water damage |
| Windstorm or hail | Collapse caused by certain perils (provided as an additional coverage) |
| Smoke | |
| Aircraft or vehicles | |
| Riot or civil commotion | |
| Vandalism | |
| Sprinkler leakage | |
| Sinkhole collapse | |
| Volcanic action | |
| Fungus, wet rot, dry rot, and bacteria (provided as an additional limited coverage) | |

[DA00449]

for losses from catastrophes such as war, nuclear reaction, and governmental action.

Most policies that provide coverage on buildings and personal property at fixed locations exclude coverage for earthquake and flood losses. An earthquake can be a catastrophe that affects many different properties in the same geographic area at the same time. Also, the extent of earthquake damage partially depends on the property's construction. A building that is susceptible to fire damage might be less susceptible to earthquake damage, and vice versa. For these and other reasons, coverage for earthquakes is excluded from most commercial property policies. Earthquake coverage can usually be added by endorsement, for an additional premium.

Flood damage also can be catastrophic and is inevitable for property in low-lying areas near rivers, creeks, or streams. Flood insurance on buildings and personal property is available through the federal government's National Flood Insurance Program (NFIP). Insurers generally are not willing to provide coverage for a loss that is certain to occur, but in certain situations, private insurers do issue flood insurance that does not involve the federal program.

Inland marine policies usually provide Special Form coverage, often without certain exclusions, such as flood and earthquake, that are typically excluded in BPP policies. In some instances, however, inland marine policies provide Basic or Broad Form coverage.

Property insurance policies also typically exclude loss from inherent vice and latent defect. Examples of inherent vice include perishable goods, such as meat or fruit, that will spoil or decay, and wood, that will warp if subject to humidity for a prolonged period. Examples of latent defect include aluminum siding that, because of a problem with the formula for the paint, begins to peel and roof shingles that deteriorate because of their chemical composition.

Other excluded perils include wear and tear and other "maintenance perils." These maintenance perils usually are not covered even in the broadest property insurance policies. Some of these excluded perils (wear and tear, marring and scratching, or rust) involve the results of ordinary use and aging rather than unexpected damage. Damage from the other perils (water seepage, insects, or rodents) is usually preventable through proper care and maintenance.

## Covered Financial Consequences

Commercial property insurance is primarily associated with coverage for the reduction in value of property (building or personal property) that has been damaged or destroyed. Commercial property insurance also can cover other financial consequences of a property loss, including lost income and **extra expenses**. The types of commercial property insurance that cover these additional financial consequences are more specifically known as business income and extra expense insurance.

Extra expenses

Expenses, in addition to ordinary expenses, that an organization incurs to mitigate the effects of a business interruption.

Business income insurance

Insurance that covers the reduction in an organization's income when operations are interrupted by damage to property caused by a covered peril.

Extra expense coverage

Insurance coverage for extra expenses incurred by the named insured to avoid or minimize the suspension of operations resulting from direct damage caused by a covered cause of loss.

**Business income insurance** covers the reduction in the organization's net income resulting from a suspension of the insured's operations because of damage by a covered cause of loss to property at the insured's location. By covering the insured's reduction in net income, business income insurance can restore the business to the financial position it would have been in had no direct loss occurred.

Business income insurance policies commonly include coverage for extra expenses, or **extra expense coverage** can be purchased in a separate form. Either way, extra expense insurance covers additional expenses incurred to reduce the length of the business interruption or that enable a business to continue some operations despite damage to its property.

For example, Iris, an insurance agent, might rent office space to conduct her business at a temporary location during the repairs to her office building following a fire. Iris's rental expense would be covered as an extra expense, as would any expenses beyond her normal expenses, such as the costs of installing telephone service and of notifying her customers of the temporary location.

### Apply Your Knowledge

MNO Company wants to buy insurance that will pay for its loss of revenue if MNO's regular business location becomes unusable because of damage by a covered cause of loss. What type of insurance does MNO need?

a. The Building and Personal Property Coverage Form

b. Business income insurance

c. Extra expense insurance

d. Inland marine insurance

*Feedback: b.* Business income insurance provides coverage for the loss of revenue resulting from a suspension of operations because of damage by a covered cause of loss to property at the insured's location.

## SUMMARY

Three important aspects of property loss exposures are the types of property that might be exposed to loss, damage, or destruction; the causes of loss; and the financial consequences of a loss. For insurance purposes, real and personal property can be classified as buildings, contents, property in transit, property in the possession of others, and floating property. Buildings and personal property are subject to many potential causes of loss, including fire, theft, windstorm, flood, earthquake, terrorism, and war. The adverse financial consequences of a property loss might include a reduction in the value of the property, lost income, or extra expenses.

Commercial property insurance policies define the property loss exposures they cover by specifying the types and locations of covered property and the covered causes of loss. The Building and Personal Property Coverage Form (BPP) is often used to insure buildings and other structures, the insured's business personal property, and the personal property of others.Inland marine insurance covers loss exposures that are excluded by the BPP, such as goods in domestic transit, property of the insured in the possession of others, and movable equipment. Commercial property insurance policies are available with Basic Form coverage, Broad Form coverage, or Special Form (open perils) coverage. Business income insurance provides coverage for lost income and/or extra expenses because of a covered direct loss to building or personal property.

## ASSIGNMENT NOTES

1. Insurance Information Institute, The III Insurance Fact Book 2011 (New York: Insurance Information Institute, 2011), pp. 128 and 132.
2. The III Insurance Fact Book 2011, p. 128.

# Direct Your Learning

9

## Commercial Liability Insurance

### Educational Objectives

After learning the content of this assignment, you should be able to:

- Identify the common liability loss exposures of commercial insureds.
- Given a description of a commercial loss exposure or a loss, determine whether it would likely be covered by any of the following types of insurance:
  - Commercial general liability insurance
  - Commercial auto insurance
  - Workers compensation and employers liability insurance
  - Commercial umbrella liability insurance

### Outline

# Commercial Liability Insurance

# 9

## COMMERCIAL LIABILITY LOSS EXPOSURES

Commercial liability loss exposures can arise from a business's premises, operations, products, completed work, automobiles, and employees.

Commercial liability loss exposures can vary substantially based on factors such as a business's type of operations, location, products or services provided, and number of employees. Some examples of commercial liability loss exposures include pollution of a waterway resulting from a chemical spill at a manufacturing plant, injuries to a purchaser of a defective product manufactured by a business, and damage to a customer's home caused by an employee-driven delivery truck.

All liability loss exposures share certain characteristics, or elements, and can be categorized by type, thus providing a framework for identifying specific commercial liability loss exposures.

### Elements of a Liability Loss Exposure

A commercial liability loss exposure presents the possibility that the business may become legally responsible for injury or damage to another party and suffer financial consequences as a result.

#### Basis for Legal Liability

Legal liability usually is based on **tort law**, but may also be based on **statutes** or contracts. The central concern of tort law is determining liability for injury or loss. The most common tort is **negligence**.

Some statutes extend, restrict, or clarify the rights of injured parties to recover compensation for their injuries. Workers compensation laws and no-fault auto laws, which grant or restrict the right of one party to recover from another, are prominent examples of such statutes.

In addition to being exposed to direct liability under tort law or statute, a business can assume, by contract, another party's liability to others. This type of contractual assumption of liability is called a **hold-harmless agreement or indemnity agreement**.

Statute

A written law passed by a legislative body, at either the federal or state level.

Tort law

The branch of civil law that deals with civil wrongs other than breaches of contract.

Negligence

The failure to exercise the degree of care that a reasonable person in a similar situation would exercise to avoid harming others.

Hold-harmless agreement (or indemnity agreement)

A contractual provision that obligates one of the parties to assume the legal liability of another party.

## Potential Financial Consequences

If a court finds that a person or an organization making a liability claim has sustained some definite injury or harm, it may require the legally liable party to pay **damages** to the injured party. The accused party might also incur costs to defend itself in court and suffer other consequences, such as loss of reputation, that have financial ramifications.

Damages
Money claimed by, or a monetary award to, a party who has suffered bodily injury or property damage for which another party is legally responsible.

# Categories of Commercial Liability Loss Exposures

Four of the most important categories of commercial liability loss exposures are premises and operations liability, products and completed operations liability, automobile liability, and workers compensation and employers liability.

## Premises and Operations Liability Loss Exposure

The premises and operations liability loss exposure entails the possibility that an organization will be held legally responsible for bodily injury to another or damage to another's property caused by either of these kinds of accidents:

- An accident occurring on premises (land, buildings, or other structures) it owns, leases, or rents
- An accident occurring away from such premises, but only if it arises out of the organization's ongoing (as opposed to completed) operations

The **premises liability exposure** arises from ownership, occupancy, or use of property (the premises). For example, an accident that could lead to a premises liability claim against an organization might involve a visitor being injured because of dangerous conditions on the premises, such as icy walkways, uneven stairs, sharp objects, unguarded machinery, insufficient security, or a fire.

Premises liability exposure
The exposure to liability for bodily injury or property damage due to the ownership, occupancy, or use of the premises.

Operations liability exposure
The exposure to liability for bodily injury or property damage resulting from the insured's ongoing business activities, as opposed to the insured's completed operations.

The **operations liability exposure** arises from an ongoing activity in addition to the occupancy of property. For example, a contractor paving a road has an operations liability exposure. If a member of the public is injured as a result of negligent construction activity that occurs while the road is being paved, any resulting liability claim against the contractor is considered to have arisen from the operations liability exposure. See the exhibit "Examples of Commercial Liability Loss Exposures."

### Examples of Commercial Liability Loss Exposures

Premises liability exposure: A customer trips on an uneven carpet in a retail store or slips on icy pavement outside the store.

Operations liability exposure: Several cars are damaged and their drivers are injured when a building contractor's crane collapses and crashes onto the street below.

[DA07512]

## Products and Completed Operations Liability Loss Exposure

Liability for products and liability for completed operations are so similar that they are usually handled jointly in commercial liability insurance. Nevertheless, products liability and completed operations liability each have distinguishing characteristics.

The **products liability exposure** relates to the potential legal liability of the manufacturer, distributor, or retailer to the user or consumer of a product because of injury or damage resulting from the product. The liability is based on the manufacture, distribution, or sale of an unsafe, dangerous, or defective product and the failure of the manufacturer, distributor, or retailer to meet the legal duties associated with that product. See the exhibit "Products Liability Loss Exposure—An Example."

**Products liability exposure**
A manufacturer's or seller's exposure to liability for harm suffered by a buyer, user, or bystander as a result of a defective product.

### Products Liability Loss Exposure—An Example

A child receives a toboggan that was purchased from a sporting goods store as a gift. The first time the child uses the toboggan, it suddenly veers off course and crashes into a tree. The child breaks several bones and requires surgery and a one-week hospital stay. The child's parent could sue both the store and the manufacturer on the child's behalf.

[DA07513]

The **completed operations liability exposure** relates to the potential legal liability of a contractor, repairer, or other entity for losses arising from the entity's completed work. For example, completed operations liability could result from a lawsuit filed against a decking construction contractor and alleging injury to persons who had been standing on a backyard wooden deck when it collapsed. See the exhibit "Elements and Categories of Commercial Liability Loss Exposures."

**Completed operations liability exposure**
The exposure to liability for bodily injury or property damage arising out of the insured's completed work.

## Automobile Liability Loss Exposure

Automobile liability consists of legal responsibility for bodily injury or property damage arising out of the ownership, maintenance, or use of automobiles (cars, trucks, trailers). Mobile equipment—such as forklifts, bulldozers, and mobile cranes—is not included in the auto liability category. The activities that create auto liability loss exposures can be classified as ownership, maintenance, and use. (Liability for the ownership, maintenance, or use of mobile equipment is customarily included in the premises and operations liability exposure.)

Simply owning an auto can be the basis for auto liability. For example, an auto owner can be held legally liable for negligent operation of the owner's auto even when the auto is operated by a borrower using the auto for his or

## Elements and Categories of Commercial Liability Loss Exposures

| Category | Description | Elements | |
|---|---|---|---|
| | | Basis for Legal Liability | Financial Consequences |
| Premises and operations | BI or PD occurring on premises or away from premises but arising out of organization's operations | Tort law and, in some cases, statutes or contracts | Damages, including medical expenses and other costs |
| Products and completed operations | BI or PD arising out of organization's products or completed work | Tort law and, in some cases, statutes or contracts | Damages, including medical expenses and other costs; possible loss of reputation |
| Automobile | BI or PD resulting from ownership, maintenance, or use of autos | Tort law and, in some cases, statutes or contracts | Damages, including medical expenses and other costs |
| Workers compensation and employers liability | BI to employees at work | WC statutes; tort law if no WC law applies | Medical costs, lost wages, and temporary or permanent disability income; damages in tort if no WC law applies |

*(BI = bodily injury; PD = property damage; WC = workers compensation)*

[DA07514]

her own purposes. Many states have enacted statutes that make an auto owner liable for operation of the auto by any person who uses the auto with the owner's permission.

Negligent maintenance of an auto can also be the basis for auto liability. For example, negligent servicing of brakes, tires, or steering apparatus may cause a truck to collide with another vehicle.

Negligent use of an auto is the most likely way a business can incur auto liability. Whether the organization's owner or an employee is driving the vehicle, the organization is generally held liable for a loss resulting from negligent use of an auto in conducting its operations.

## Workers Compensation and Employers Liability Loss Exposure

Workers compensation and employers liability are separate, but related, exposures that result from the possibility that an employee might be injured at work. Such injury can be the result of a single accident or long-term exposure to harmful conditions (occupational disease).

An employer's responsibility to pay claims under workers compensation statutes is a common example of liability imposed by statute. The term "workers compensation statutes" includes the various state workers compensation statutes as well as similar federal statutes that apply to certain types of employees, such as maritime employees. Workers compensation statutes require employers to pay certain benefits to employees who suffer an occupational injury or disease. These benefits include medical costs, lost wages, and temporary or permanent disability income.

In addition to being liable to pay statutory benefits, an employer has an employers liability exposure for tort suits as a result of occupational injury or disease to its employees in two general situations. The first situation occurs when the injured employee is covered by a workers compensation statute but the particular injury (such as intentional injury committed by the employer) is one for which the law has nevertheless permitted tort suits. The second situation occurs when the injured employee (such as a farm worker or a casual employee) is not covered by a workers compensation statute.

# COMMERCIAL LIABILITY COVERAGES

The financial consequences of a liability loss can be devastating to a business organization. Business owners can protect themselves from such consequences by identifying their liability loss exposures and purchasing the appropriate insurance coverage.

Any organization, whether operating for-profit or not-for-profit, faces a variety of liability loss exposures that could cause the organization to fail. One way for organizations to manage liability loss exposures is to transfer the financial consequences of those exposures to an insurer by purchasing commercial liability insurance. Four common types of commercial liability insurance are general liability insurance, commercial auto insurance, workers compensation and employers liability insurance, and umbrella liability insurance.

## Commercial General Liability Insurance

Commercial general liability (CGL) insurance is the foundation for most organizations' liability insurance programs. The most commonly used standard form for providing CGL insurance is the **Commercial General Liability Coverage Form** of Insurance Services Office, Inc. (ISO), an insurance advisory organization. The CGL coverage form provides three separate coverages:

- Coverage A—Bodily Injury and Property Damage Liability
- Coverage B—Personal and Advertising Injury Liability
- Coverage C—Medical Payments

**Commercial General Liability Coverage Form**
A coverage form commonly used for insuring an organization's premises and operations liability loss exposures and products and completed operations liability loss exposures.

## Coverage A—Bodily Injury and Property Damage Liability

In Coverage A of the CGL, the insurer agrees to pay those sums that the insured becomes legally obligated to pay as damages because of bodily injury or property damage to which the insurance applies. The insurer also agrees to defend the insured against claims or suits seeking damages covered under the policy.

As defined in the CGL, bodily injury includes bodily injury, sickness, disease, or death; and property damage means physical injury to property and resulting loss of use of that property, or loss of use of property that is not physically injured.

Subject to applicable exclusions and conditions, Coverage A insures two general categories of loss exposures:

- Premises and operations liability
- Products and completed operations liability

The premises and operations liability loss exposure entails the possibility that an organization will be held liable because of bodily injury or property damage caused either by an accident occurring on premises (land, buildings, or other structures) owned, leased, or rented by the organization, or caused by an accident occurring away from such premises, but only if it arises out of the organization's ongoing (as opposed to completed) operations.

The products and completed operations liability loss exposure entails the possibility that an organization will be held liable because of bodily injury or property damage arising out of products sold or distributed by the insured or arising out of operations that the insured has completed or abandoned.

## Coverage B—Personal and Advertising Injury Liability

Personal and advertising injury limit

The most the insurer will pay under Coverage B for the sum of all personal and advertising injury to one person or organization.

Libel

A defamatory statement expressed in a writing.

Slander

A defamatory statement expressed by speech.

False arrest

The seizure or forcible restraint of a person without legal authority.

In Coverage B of the CGL, the insurer agrees to pay those sums that the insured becomes legally obligated to pay as damages because of **personal and advertising injury** to which the insurance applies. The insurer also agrees to defend the insured against claims or suits seeking damages covered under the policy.

As defined in the CGL, personal and advertising injury means injury arising out of any of several specified offenses (torts) that could be committed in the course of the insured's operations or advertising activities. Examples of such offenses are **libel**, **slander**, **false arrest**, and use of another's advertising idea. In this definition, the word "injury" is not defined by the policy but takes its usual broad meaning. It therefore includes, for example, injury to financial condition, injury to reputation, and psychological injury. The policy states that personal and advertising injury even includes bodily injury that results from one of the specified offenses, such as bodily injury resulting from false arrest.

## Coverage C—Medical Payments

In Coverage C of the CGL, the insurer agrees to pay medical expenses for bodily injury caused by an accident occurring on the insured's premises. The insurer also agrees to pay medical expenses for bodily injury caused by an accident that occurs away from the insured's premises (for example, at a job site where the insured is working) if the accident results from the named insured's operations.

Medical payments coverage pays regardless of whether the insured is legally liable. Therefore, it is not technically liability insurance, even though it is commonly included in liability insurance policies.

The purpose of medical payments coverage is to provide a modest amount of insurance for settling minor injury cases without requiring a determination of liability. In that sense, the coverage provides a means of making prompt settlements, satisfying potential liability claimants, and avoiding possibly larger liability claims.

# Commercial Auto Insurance

CGL policies exclude most auto liability exposures. Consequently, an organization that uses autos also needs liability insurance for the ownership, maintenance, or use of those autos. The **Business Auto Coverage Form**, another ISO standard form, is widely used to meet the auto liability insurance needs of most organizations. These organizations may also use this form for other auto coverages, such as auto physical damage, auto medical payments, and uninsured motorists.

Business Auto Coverage Form

A coverage form, filed by ISO, that covers liability arising out of the ownership, maintenance, or use of autos and physical damage to autos owned, leased, or hired by the named insured.

In the Business Auto Coverage Form's auto liability section, the insurer agrees to pay all sums the insured legally must pay as damages because of bodily injury or property damage to which the insurance applies caused by an accident and resulting from the ownership, maintenance, or use of a covered auto. The insurer also agrees to defend the insured against any claim or suit alleging damages that would be covered under the policy.

"Ownership, maintenance, or use" of an auto includes virtually any activity involving a covered auto for which an insured might be held liable, including these kinds of liability:

- Liability as an owner of the auto
- Liability for injury resulting from faulty maintenance of the auto
- Liability for use or operation of the auto by the insured organization

The insured indicates the categories of autos it wishes the policy to cover by selecting numerical symbols in the policy. Covered autos for liability insurance can include autos owned, leased, or hired by the named insured, as well as autos the insured does not own, lease, or hire but that are used on the insured's behalf (such as an employee using his or her own auto on the insured's business).

## Workers Compensation and Employers Liability Insurance

**Workers compensation and employers liability insurance**
Insurance that covers (1) benefits an employer is obligated to pay under workers compensation laws and (2) employee injury claims made against the employer that are not covered by workers compensation laws.

**Workers compensation statute**
A statute that obligates employers, regardless of fault, to pay specified medical, disability, rehabilitation, and death benefits for their employees' job-related injuries and diseases.

**Workers Compensation and Employers Liability Insurance Policy (WC&EL policy)**
The policy used in most states to provide workers compensation and employers liability insurance.

Almost all employers purchase **workers compensation and employers liability insurance** to cover these loss exposures:

- The insured's obligation to pay benefits required by a **workers compensation statute**
- The insured's liability to pay damages because of injury to the insured's employees as a result of a claim or suit based on legal grounds other than a workers compensation statute

Workers compensation statutes exist in all states and other jurisdictions of the United States, every Canadian province, and some other nations. These laws, in return for removing the right of injured employees to sue their employers for occupational injury, obligate employers to compensate injured employees regardless of whether their injuries resulted from the employer's negligence. The workers compensation system is designed to provide injured workers prompt payment while reducing costs and court workloads that arise from litigation. Workers compensation statutes apply to almost all types of private employment. Large employers can self-insure in some instances, but most employers buy workers compensation insurance that will pay injured workers the benefits required by law.

In most of the U.S., workers compensation and employers liability insurance is provided under a standard form known as the **Workers Compensation and Employers Liability Insurance Policy (WC&EL Policy)** developed by the National Council on Compensation Insurance (NCCI), an insurance advisory organization. The WC&EL policy provides its two basic coverages in these coverage sections:

- Part 1—Workers Compensation Insurance
- Part 2—Employers Liability Insurance

### Part 1—Workers Compensation Insurance

In Part 1—Workers Compensation Insurance, the insurer agrees to pay promptly when due the benefits required of the insured by the workers compensation law of any state listed in the policy's Information Page.

Workers compensation laws usually require these benefits:

- Unlimited medical expense benefits for a covered injury or disease
- Disability income benefits, which compensate an injured employee for wage loss due to a covered injury or disease

- Rehabilitation benefits, which include expenses for complete medical rehabilitation (and sometimes vocational rehabilitation) following a covered injury or disease
- Death benefits, which include a flat amount for burial expenses as well as partial replacement of the worker's former weekly wage

### Part 2—Employers Liability Insurance

In Part 2—Employers Liability Insurance, the insurer agrees to pay all sums the insured legally must pay as damages because of bodily injury to the insured's employees, provided the bodily injury is covered by the Employers Liability Insurance section. Because employers liability insurance excludes any obligation imposed by a workers compensation or similar law, most occupational injuries and illnesses are covered under Part 1—Workers Compensation Insurance.

An example of a claim that could be covered under employers liability insurance is a bodily injury claim made by an employee whose occupation (such as farm work) is not covered by the applicable workers compensation law. Another example is a lawsuit by an employee's spouse for loss of services (such as companionship and help with household duties) because of the employee's injuries. The spouse's damages would not be covered under workers compensation insurance.

## Commercial Umbrella Liability Insurance

A commercial umbrella liability policy provides limits of insurance that apply in addition to the limits of the insured's primary liability policies, including CGL, commercial auto, employers liability, and possibly other liability policies. Umbrella liability coverage is also referred to as "excess" coverage because it applies in excess of the primary coverages.

Insureds need umbrella or excess liability coverage because the maximum loss for most liability exposures cannot easily be estimated. Awards to injured persons can, in some cases, reach extremely high totals. For example, hundreds of verdicts in excess of $1 million are made each year in the U.S. Although most organizations are not likely to experience such losses, the possibility of a large liability loss exists for virtually any business.

Umbrella liability coverage becomes applicable when the amount of damages for which the insured is liable exceeds the limit of an underlying policy. Umbrella policies may also cover, on a primary basis, some claims that are not covered at all by the underlying policy or policies. Such coverage is often referred to as "**drop-down coverage.**" Each insurer writing umbrella liability policies has its own requirements for the types and amounts of underlying insurance that the insured must have.

**Drop-down coverage**

Coverage provided by many umbrella liability policies for (1) claims not covered at all by the underlying policies and (2) claims that are not covered by an underlying policy only because the underlying policy's aggregate limits have been depleted.

## *Apply Your Knowledge*

Kate, a customer of Real Estate Broker (REB), was injured when she slipped and fell on a wet hallway floor in REB's office. Kate's losses resulting from the accident consisted of $5,000 in medical expenses and $30,000 in lost wages. Assuming that REB was legally liable for Kate's losses, which one of REB's coverages would be the most likely to cover REB's liability to Kate?

a. Commercial general liability

b. Commercial auto

c. Workers compensation and employers liability

d. Commercial umbrella

*Feedback: a.* Commercial general liability coverage would most likely cover Kate's injuries. CGL's Coverage A—Bodily Injury and Property Damage Liability covers sums that REB is legally obligated to pay to Kate as damages because it was at fault for the accident. These damages include both Kate's medical expenses and her lost wages. Under Coverage A, the insurer would also provide legal defense for REB in relation to the claim. Coverage C—Medical Payments would also apply to Kate's medical costs, but the limit of that coverage would likely be inadequate to cover all of those costs.

# SUMMARY

A liability loss exposure entails the possibility of one party becoming legally liable for injury or harm to another party. The elements of a liability loss exposure include the basis for legal liability (torts or statutes) and the potential financial consequences of liability loss exposures (damages, defense costs, and damage to reputation). Four common categories of commercial liability loss exposures are premises and operations liability, products and completed operations liability, automobile liability, and workers compensation and employers liability.

Four common types of commercial liability insurance are general liability insurance, commercial auto insurance, workers compensation and employers liability insurance, and umbrella liability insurance. Commercial general liability insurance covers premises, operations, products, and completed operations loss exposures. Commercial auto insurance covers the ownership, maintenance, or use of a business's autos. Workers compensation and employers liability insurance pays injured workers the benefits required by workers compensation laws and, in cases to which workers compensation laws do not apply, covers insured employers in the event of lawsuits brought by employees for occupational injuries or diseases. An umbrella liability policy provides excess coverage over liability policies and may also cover, on a primary basis, some claims that are not covered at all by the underlying policies.

# Index

Page numbers in boldface refer to pages where the word or phrase is defined.

# T



# U



# W